TABLE O

The Craziest Instruction God Ever Gave Me
ISBN 1-56394-217-8
Copyright © 2002 by *MIKE MURDOCK*
All publishing rights belong exclusively to Wisdom International
Published by The Wisdom Center
P. O. Box 99 · Denton, Texas 76202
1-888-WISDOM-1 (1-888-947-3661)
Website: www.thewisdomcenter.tv

WHY I WROTE THIS BOOK

Little Hinges Swing Great Doors.
Small keys open bank vaults.

Sometimes, our perception is that small changes will require a gigantic and dramatic truth or discovery. Often, we feel that some incredible effort must be exerted...extreme discipline rallied from our innermost being...before we can experience something glorious and wonderful.

The opposite is true.

Just as the rudder controls the ship...the small key unlocks a huge bank vault with great treasures... the smallest act of obedience can launch a parade of miracles that will outlast your own lifetime.

Millions live on the desert of loneliness and helplessness because they do not understand this truth. Their memories of failures have birthed deep emotions of helplessness, weakness and indescribable inferiority. As they continuously replay past memories of lost dreams...events that were not changed...miracles that were not received or experienced. The victim mindset is birthed. Then, it becomes strengthened. Then, the victim vocabulary and viewpoint become the lifestyle and way of life for millions.

The smallest movement could dramatically effect a miracle change...beyond your imagination.

Scripturally, it is proven repeatedly. The blind man who had lived in darkness from his youth, simply cried out and experienced the instant healing power of Jesus. A simple cry.

The woman who had an issue of blood for 12 years had spent everything she had on doctors. The best physicians, the most advanced tests and the accumulated discoveries of mankind...left her helpless and hopeless.

But, she reached...pursued...to touch the hem of the robe of Jesus.

What 4,000 years of discoveries could not produce...her simple pursuit to touch Jesus birthed that miracle.

Great Changes Do Not Always Require Great Effort.

Your reading this very book seems like a simple act, a very simple task. You may even be reading this book while waiting to catch a plane, see your doctor or for your mate to finish getting dressed.

Yet, you have already birthed your next season of miracles...by being humble enough to reach for Wisdom.

The Proof Of Humility Is The Willingness To Reach.

The Product Of Humility Is The Ability To Change.

You will read a very illogical testimony of my life. You will discover that the smallest act of obedience is a monument in the mind of God.

How do you impress a God Who has seen everything?

You do something He does not see often.

My greatest discovery about God is quite simple: God's Only Pain Is To Be Doubted; God's Only

Pleasure Is To Be Believed.

Your dream can come true.

Your greatest goals can be achieved.

You do not have to live another day without a miracle.

Helping you birth your miracle matters to me.

That's why I wrote this book.

-DR. MIKE MURDOCK

Warfare Always Surrounds The Birth Of A Miracle.

-MIKE MURDOCK

❧ 1 ❧

YOU WILL ALWAYS NEED A MIRACLE.

―――――▸◦◂―――――

Miracles Are Necessary In God's World.

God did not create a world that could survive without His presence, His power or His peace. Any automobile company knows that parts will be needed, breakdowns will occur. Thousands of mechanics have jobs because that automobile will need extra attention. Accidents will occur. Breakdowns will happen.

Likewise, the Creator of this universe knew that His family would need the miraculous, the extraordinary and the uncommon events to happen in their life...for many reasons.

Everything God created has a downside. Nothing He created is complete. Nothing. Your eyes need a view. Your ears need sound. Your mind needs thoughts. Your mouth requires words. Your feet require land to walk on. Everything created requires a connection for its completion and fulfillment.

Each of us continues to struggle for completion... arrival...fulfillment. Singles look around a room of hundreds and think, "If I were just married, my life would be complete." In the same room, hundreds of married people look around and think, "Look at all the singles. Freedom, freedom, freedom!" The childless couple thinks, "If we just had a child, our life would be complete. Our home!" When you gaze on the countenance of a woman who has had six or seven children, you don't always see fulfillment though, do you? Sometimes you see a look of survival...or, "Just a few more years, and they'll be grown up and out of the house!"

If you marry someone who is extremely passionate, you may discover they have a dangerous side to them as well. If you marry someone who brings you flowers every week, you may discover them bringing somebody else flowers as well on their job! If you marry a man who loves to work, you may discover the downside of that...he doesn't want to come home!

God left something out of everything He created...Himself. Many religions have been based on the supposition that God Himself is in everything He created. In a sense, it could be true that His presence, views, imprint is left like an artist and his painting.

But, the Creator is not His creation.

The artist is not his painting.

The mother is not her child.

The distinction must be discerned, perceived and respected.

Some years ago, I kept seeing pictures in magazines of people standing on their boats. The beautiful water, hair blowing in the breeze and the aura of abandonment intrigued me. I thought people who own boats are happy people.

So, when I received a large royalty check, I invested in a beautiful boat. I consulted nobody. I knew it was going to be the key to the next season of joy in my personal life. I imagined being out on the water, relaxing, reading a book...in my own boat. Nobody explained to me the cost of upkeep, maintenance, a boat slip, repairs that would be continuously necessary. My friends wanted to use my boat. So, I allowed it. One friend wrecked the boat. When I stopped loaning it to them afterwards, they became angry and sullen toward me.

So, I sold my boat.

There is a downside to everything.

I decided to purchase a limousine with my boat money. I have always loved limousines. For some reason, I always felt very special riding in the back of a limousine, feeling luxurious, relaxed and "being pampered." My limousine was beautiful...long, white. I was so proud of it. Then, it dawned on me that I didn't have a chauffeur! Believe me, it's no fun driving your own limousine around...alone! So, I began to attempt to find someone to drive me various places, shopping, restaurants, appointments, and so forth.

Who would I be comfortable enough with to share all of that information with? Now, discretion, confidentiality and privacy became another issue. My life is connected with well-known ministers, personalities and who some would call celebrities. So, I could not meet a famous person for a meal without exposing that appointment to this chauffeur...who in turn had another circle of friends...who trusted another circle of friends. It changed the entire picture. It eventually dawned on me, too, that the windows were shaded anyhow and nobody knew you were in it...so the fun was an inside "head job!"

I sold my limousine. *There's a downside to*

everything.

I bought four horses. Beautiful horses. One was a Palomino, looking like Trigger, the horse that belonged to Roy Rogers. One of the horses was a beautiful Indian Paint that I was quite proud of. One was an Arabian beauty. Oh, I was so proud of the environment I had sculptured for myself here at my home. I soon discovered the responsibility of taking care of these horses. My veterinarian bill for one month was $2,000! When I was gone for two weeks, I brought some friends on the property to see my horses. Proudly, I strolled over boldly to my beautiful Palomino I had just purchased. It proceeded to snap and bite at my hand. Horses require affection and attention...continually. I did not know that. I had watched too many Clint Eastwood movies, read too many Louie Lamour books. I thought horses were beautiful, loyal companions that would come running to your side when they heard your unique and cherished whistle. In fact, I thought horses could not enjoy life without their owner walking by their side. Loafing sheds, barns, feeding all became a part of the ritual and daily routine. Studying the uniqueness of each horse and what was expected and required. When you buy four horses, you have to purchase four shovels as well!

I sold my horses.

There's a downside to everything.

I purchased a beautiful zebra to join my menagerie of animals. I had five deer, llamas and many other animals around at the time. I had spent a total of a year in East Africa and loved the atmosphere of exotic animals. The safari atmosphere stimulated my imagination. At the time, 25 peacocks were on my property as well. (That is another story within itself. Always enjoy the feathers spread! That's the only delightful thing in owning peacocks!)

Here was my plan: When I opened the gates after a long journey home, my house and property would look like a scene from East Africa. I imagined it continually—the zebra grazing among the deer. The peacocks with their feathers spread. So, after a long series of meetings in California, I flew all night to my house. After getting out of the car, I started walking around my property, viewing my animals. The time was 6:30 a.m. in the morning. I had flown all night long. While watching my zebra with great pride, he suddenly lifted his head. He began pawing, and I watched with shock as he headed toward me in a direct frontal attack.

I could hardly believe what I was seeing. I grabbed a long board to keep his head at bay. Truly, I would have won America's Funniest Video Award as I held off this wild animal long enough to open the gate and get back outside. The gate closed just in time to separate us. Picture this—I am standing on the outside of my gate facing my home. The zebra is inside the gate, daring me to enter my own premises. It was a sight I was not soon to forget.

By the way, if you have ever wondered where the demons went after they left the pigs under the instruction of Jesus, they probably went into zebras! Of that, I am certain. At any rate, I sold the zebra to some men over in Fort Worth the next week. They called me a few days later and said, "He has almost killed two of our cowboys!"

"I know," I replied. "He almost killed me! That's why I sold him!"

Yes, I sold my zebra. *There's a downside to everything.*

I have always loved monkeys. When I go to zoos, watching monkeys is one of my favorite pastimes. From the time I was a child, I always wanted to own a monkey. I imagined it would be my favorite pet, going with me everywhere. So, it was a delightful day when the little spider monkey clung to me as a little baby. I changed its diapers every two hours. Let me say one thing about owning a monkey: owning a monkey is like having a child without any hope of an improvement. The monkey required attention continuously. I did not really have facilities to house it properly, but the caretaker of our property soon found that the monkey could unlock almost any door or gate it was around. It had one goal—to outwit anyone around it. It was an exhausting experience...not an exhilarating experience.

I sold my monkey. *There's a downside to everything.*

It's quite simple—God never gives us gifts to replace His presence in our lives.

God will never give you anything that will bring fulfillment and satisfaction to you. You were created for His presence.

Birds require air.

Fish require water.

You require His presence...for your contentment and completion.

I feel that God gives us gifts for three basic reasons:

1. *To Establish A Path To Himself As Our Source.* Remember the childhood story where Hansel and Gretal left crumbs along the path...so they could be found later? God gives us gifts to provoke a desire to pursue Him, the Source of all things.

2. *To Reveal His Nature As A Giver.* Psalm 84:11, "...no good thing will He withhold from them that walk uprightly." Jesus had a fascinating picture when He said, "Or what man is there of you, whom if his son ask bread, will he give him a stone? Or if he ask a fish, will he give him a serpent? If ye then, being evil, know how to give good gifts unto your children, how much more shall your Father which is in heaven give good things to them that ask him?" (Matt. 7:9-11). He wants pursuit. Jesus instructed us to ask, "Ask, and it shall be given you; seek, and ye shall find; knock, and it shall be opened unto you: For every one that asketh receiveth; and he that seeketh findeth; and to him that knocketh it shall be opened" (Matt. 7:7-8).

3. *To Give Us The Opportunity To Become Givers Like Himself, Thus Experiencing The Feelings God Experiences In Being God.*

Men hoard.

Satan steals.

God gives.

God gives us gifts so we can do exactly what He does...giving...to experience what it is like to be God!

Yes, you will always need a miracle while you are on the earth. The richest men on earth would pay millions for their baby to be healed from an incurable disease. Some of the most beautiful women on earth would give up their beauty to be able to trust the faithfulness of their mate to them. Some of the most productive intellectual giants live with the throbbing heartache of a loved one who did not respond to their love. Everyone experiences being unloved at some point in their life.

You cannot sustain any environment for any length of time...that will not require the miracle intervention of a miracle God.

God created a world that would *need* Him.

That's part of His genius in being God.

A needy world provides God one of His greatest pleasures...the pleasure of being pursued and desired and ultimately chosen.

2

WHEN YOU ASK GOD FOR A MIRACLE, HE WILL ALWAYS GIVE YOU AN INSTRUCTION.

Asking Is Necessary For Receiving.

Jesus knew this. That is why He emphasized to everyone that He taught that asking was necessary for receiving, seeking was necessary for finding, knocking was necessary for the door to be opened. I mentioned earlier, The Proof Of Humility Is The Willingness To Reach.

Israel needed a miracle. They faced a very formidable foe, the town of Jericho. It was surrounded by walls that seemed impenetrable. As Joshua sought God for counsel, God gave him a supernatural formula. He was to walk around the walls of Jericho seven days in a row...then, seven times on Sunday. God gave him something to do.

When He healed the blind man, *He gave him an instruction.*

"When He had thus spoken, He spat on the ground, and made clay of the spittle, and He anointed the eyes of the blind man with the clay, And said unto

him, Go, wash in the pool of Siloam, (which is by inter-
pretation, Sent.) He went his way therefore, and
washed, and came seeing" (Jn. 9:6-7).

A theologian wrote that this involved walking
two miles to the pool of Siloam before he could wash it
off. That's how far he was from where Jesus told him
to wash.

"And fear not them which kill the body, but are
not able to kill the soul: but rather fear Him which is
able to destroy both soul and body in hell. Are not two
sparrows sold for a farthing? and one of them shall
not fall on the ground without your Father. But the
very hairs of your head are all numbered. Fear ye not
therefore, ye are of more value than many sparrows"
(Matt. 10:28-31).

Picture thousands of people on the hillside. Jesus
taught for several days. The people fasted the entire
time Jesus taught. Nobody left for lunch, supper or
breakfast. It's an arresting scenario. Then, the truth
emerges, "The people are very hungry." The same
Jesus who stilled the water...He suddenly gives *them*
an instruction. He asked *them* to bring the little boy's
lunch to Him...then He had *them* to sit everyone down
in groups of 50's and 100's. Then, He broke the bread.
He gave them an instruction...*something to do.*

When You Ask God For A Miracle, He Will Give
You An Instruction.

The first miracle of Jesus occurred at the
marriage of Cana. They ran out of wine. Mary, the
mother of Jesus, ignored Jesus' statement that it was
not His time to perform miracles.

"And when they wanted wine, the mother of Jesus
saith unto Him, They have no wine. Jesus saith unto

her, Woman, what have I to do with thee? Mine hour is not yet come. His mother saith unto the servants, Whatsoever He saith unto you, do it" (Jn. 2:3-5).

Jesus then gave them *an instruction*—"Jesus saith unto them, Fill the waterpots with water. And they filled them up to the brim. And He saith unto them, Draw out now, and bear unto the governor of the feast. And they bare it" (Jn. 2:7-8).

Interesting. When they asked Him for a miracle, He required a specific action *necessary* to unlock *His* supernatural involvement.

There is a Divine and awesome reason for this. I'm sure there are many reasons we do not know, but there is one that stands out to me graphically.

It is so true—When You Do The Possible, God Will Always Do The Impossible.

God never requires you to do something impossible. *Ever.*

Some years ago, a woman rushed up to me after service and said, "God just spoke to me to do something that's impossible for me to do! What should I do?"

I replied, teasingly, "Write a book! You are the first person in history that we know of that God ever required to do something impossible." Throughout the Scriptures, the only instructions God ever gave were tasks or actions that anyone in the world could do. Anyone.

Why does God give you instructions?

Does He fear our laziness? Does He fear that we are not getting things done? Is His supernatural per-formances impossible without our participation? Of course not.

The most powerful truth I've discovered about God is this:

His Only Pain Is To Be Doubted.

His Only Pleasure Is To Be Believed.

That is my single greatest discovery about the awesome Creator of this universe. He explains Himself throughout Scripture graphically, clearly and without confusion. "But without faith it is impossible to please Him; for he that cometh to God must believe that He is, and that He is a rewarder of them that diligently seek Him" (Heb. 11:6).

Faith is confidence in God. God wants to be believed. His desperation or passion to be trusted is so fierce and so strong that He forbids anyone to even enter Heaven without using their faith. He will not even forgive your sins...unless you believe Him, trust Him, have confidence in Him.

"That if thou shalt confess with thy mouth the Lord Jesus, and shalt believe in thine heart that God hath raised Him from the dead, thou shalt be saved. For with the heart man believeth unto righteousness; and with the mouth confession is made unto salvation" (Rom. 10:9-10).

God has an obsession. That obsession is to be believed and trusted...*completely.*

Doubt is His enemy. Doubt is faith in satan, the fallen angel He removed from His Heaven. How deadly is doubt to God? After nurturing the deliverance of the Israelites from Egypt, for more than 40 years, He watched them die in the wilderness without their victory...simply because they doubted Him.

God does not respond to pain. Few have grasped

this.

God does not respond to tears nor heartache.

The ungodly world has great difficulty in understanding this characteristic of God. Millions find it incompatible with the teaching that "God is love." If God really loves me, He will respond when I hurt. Not true.

God only responds to faith.

Your needs do not attract the hand of God.

Your pain is not a magnet for supernatural involvement in your life.

If you do not grasp any other truth about God, His laws or His world, it is extremely important that you grasp and understand this basic law of miracles: God Only Responds Favorably To An Act Of Faith And Confidence In Him.

This explains why His instructions are always illogical.

Walk around the walls of Jericho seven days in a row? Walking never produced miracles before. Why now? Go find the waterpots...for the creation of new wine at the marriage of Cana? Was there magic to those waterpots? Of course not. They were simple clay waterpots. Obeying His instructions documented their faith in His words.

When You Follow An Instruction, You Document Your Confidence In The Instructor.

God does not give you a miracle because you need it; God gives you a miracle as a reward for trusting Him.

I know many people who *need* miracles...and *never* experience them. I know others who continuously experience a parade of miracles...because they are always expressing their expectations of His response.

The proof that God does not respond to needs and pain prevails through Scripture. One inch from the robe of Christ, the woman who had hemorrhaged for 12 years still did not receive her miracle. She had to touch Him. Notice—Jesus did not touch her. She touched Jesus.

Jesus planned to walk past the blind man. He called out. Others angrily told him to shut up and keep quiet. He refused. He cried out until He got a response from Jesus. He pursued Jesus and experienced the miraculous.

> ▶ You Have No Right To Anything You Have Not Pursued.
> ▶ The First Proof Of Desire Is Pursuit.
> ▶ The Proof Of Faith Is Continued Pursuit.

I have watched healing ministries over the years. One minister told a woman to stand on her Bible. It seemed absurd. In a crowd of thousands, she stood on her Bible...and experienced her miracle. One healing evangelist instructed a man to run around the building after he prayed for him. The man almost refused. As he began to run around the building, he received his healing.

God is passionate about being trusted and believed. The first sin ever committed was the rebellion of satan. He did not believe God, nor in the power of God, nor in the authority of God. The first sin was possibly...the Sin of Doubt...in the greatness of God. Doubt births Unthankfulness.

Unthankfulness births Rebellion.

Rebellion births Loss.

God created everything for His personal pleasure. "Thou art worthy, O Lord, to receive glory and honour and power: for Thou hast created all things, and for Thy pleasure they are and were created" (Rev. 4:11).

God has a need to experience pleasure. That's why He creates scenarios that will require your faith and confidence in Him...before you can experience your miracle.

The focus of God is not...your miracle experience.

The focus of God...is for your faith to create His pleasure.

When You Ask God For A Miracle...He Will Give You An Instruction.

When God Gives You An Instruction, It Will Always Be Illogical To Your Natural Mind.

One Hour
In The Presence Of God
Will Reveal Any Flaw
In Your Most
Carefully Laid Plan.

-MIKE MURDOCK

❧ 3 ❧

MY PERSONAL BACKGROUND IN THE WORLD OF FAITH.

━━━➤-O-◄━━━

I have enjoyed God immensely.

My father is 85 years old. He was a pastor for over 63 years. He is also the father of seven children. He taught me to pursue God...through His personal example each day.

My father always had a separate room for prayer. Several children might sleep in the same bedroom... but, Daddy always had his own personal prayer place. Daddy never taught a lot about prayer. He simply prayed a lot...all the time.

In my mind, I have seen my father more on his knees than I have seen Him off his knees. He has easily prayed six to ten hours every day of his life. I remember one trip that I took to Africa. He went with me. Late one night, it was midnight as I turned the light off. He was there kneeling, praying quietly beside his bed. I woke up five-and-a-half hours later at 5:30 a.m. I looked across to his bed. He was still on his knees, praying. That's the way I was raised. I was raised by an intercessor. As I mentioned in my book, "The Holy Spirit Handbook," throughout my entire life, I have never heard my father curse, lie or say a single word that could not be printed on the front of any newspaper in the world.

My mother insisted that we memorize a Scripture every morning before school. Many times, I was exasperated as she made my schoolmates stand there in the living room while we all "memorized the Scripture for the day." I was embarrassed, agitated, but eventually persuaded that the word of God was the most important book in the world.

When I was two-and-a-half years old, my body was eaten up with worms. In one day alone, I vomited and passed over 600 worms. My mother chose to count them that day...for the sake of the baby book entry! The doctors did not want my case. They knew I would die. But, my father went to prayer. He has talked often about seeing my little body in the hands of satan. As he prayed, he cried out with fervor and passion, "Thou art a mighty God! Thou art a mighty God!" As he cried out for my healing, he saw in his mind a picture. It was as if Jesus walked over and took my little form out of the hands of satan and picked me up Himself. He said, "Son, it was quite simple. Jesus did not scream at satan. He said nothing to satan. It was a simple picture in my mind as I saw Jesus go take you out of the hands of satan unto Himself." The next day I was dramatically and instantly healed...and started to eat again, and so forth.

My father pioneered a new church in Franklin, Louisiana. We had no guarantee of support. Several of us children needed constant attention, nourishment and clothes...but my daddy would work every day building the church, board by board. Men he had never met in his life would drop by the property, walk over and hand him a check. He lived by his faith in God. My father never asked a church board what his salary would be. He always told me, "Son, if God wants me somewhere, that's the place I should be. It doesn't matter what the church wants to pay me. God is my Source for everything."

The purpose in my sharing this little personal testimony is to show you that my background is one of faith in God. That's what I have seen my entire life. My father's goal was to...*trust God.*

I asked him one day, "Daddy, how in the world did you and mother survive with us seven children and keep your joy?"

"Son, I have always believed the Scriptures. And the Scriptures say that children are a heritage of the Lord. So, it is my belief that your children are actual gifts from God Himself to you. Knowing that, I lived with that thankfulness for my family," he explained.

My Father's complete trust in the Integrity of God is the world I grew up in.

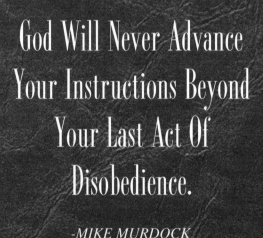

God Will Never Advance
Your Instructions Beyond
Your Last Act Of
Disobedience.

-MIKE MURDOCK

4

THE CRAZIEST INSTRUCTION CAN OFTEN PRODUCE THE GREATEST RESULTS.

It actually started in Tulsa, Oklahoma.

Tulsa is a great city in a great state. I have found Tulsa to be so affected by influence of Oral Robert's anointing that it is almost shocking. When you drive into Tulsa, you literally feel the atmosphere of the Divine touch of God on it. It is where a number of great ministries have developed since Brother Oral Roberts moved there many years ago.

Oral Roberts' own faith in God is legendary. His own revelation of the Holy Spirit has affected my life radically. His understanding of the Law of the Seed has revolutionized the prosperity of millions. Only eternity will reveal the countless miracles that have happened because of his faith in God. His son, Richard Roberts, respecting that same anointing, has received it as well and his own ministry has touched millions throughout the world. How many of us thank God for the incredible ministry of Richard and Lindsay Roberts today.

A number of years ago, I was sitting in an airport in Tulsa, Oklahoma, waiting for bad weather to subside. Every airline had been canceled for eight hours. Remembering an idea I had carried for sometime, I pulled out my black legal pad notebook and proceeded to write down every Scripture from Genesis through Revelation that contained some kind of blessing or promise.

My goal was to create a book without any other Scripture except the blessing Scriptures...in the sequence that they were recorded in the Bible. It would reveal the stream of blessings that God had created to flow into mankind...in every single book of the Bible. At that time, it never occurred to me to see exactly how many kinds of blessings were obvious.

That book later become known as the best selling, "The Blessing Book." Tens of thousands were sold through other ministries.

Approximately two years later, I sat on a platform in Washington, DC. My pastor friend was receiving the church tithe and offerings. As I was sitting there, contemplating the amount I should sow, the Holy Spirit nudged me softly with a question, "How many kinds of blessings are there in My Word?" I remembered my special study. "Fifty-eight," I replied inside my spirit. (Now, there's probably a lot more than 58, but that's how many I counted personally.)

"Plant a special Seed of $58 into this offering today. It will become a memory in the mind of God and will be a monument to your faith that you want to stand in covenant with your God for the entire 58 kinds of blessings to occur during your lifetime."

It sounded utterly ridiculous to me. Nobody

heard it. It was so strong, I remember looking around and wondering if anybody had felt or sensed what was going on inside me.

I have always known that certain numbers were important to God. He is always specific and always illogical...whether it is dealing with Gideon's 300... instructing the Israelites to walk around the walls of Jericho seven consecutive days and seven times around on the seventh day...or the prophet telling the leper to dip seven times in Jordan. Numbers do matter. Obviously, they do not seem to matter to us... but, to the One who gave us the instruction, they do.

I wrote out a special Seed for $58 immediately. Suddenly, the Holy Spirit whispered again, "Plant a special Seed of $58 for your son, Jason. It will represent that you are in covenant...that I will honor your son and bless him in his life likewise."

My mind began to dig for scriptural validation. *Was it my personal imagination?* It never lingered long in my heart for that consideration as I lived con-tinuously in relationship and communion with the Holy Spirit.

It never took me long to recognize my mother's voice on the telephone.

Relationship really makes a difference.

That's why I never get into an argument with people concerning whether God spoke to me or not. If He spoke to me, it doesn't make any difference whether they believe it or not.

I wrote out a second Seed-faith gift of $58 and, this time I placed Jason's name on it specifically. I gave my Seed *an Assignment.*

I believe that giving money as a trade out for a

miracle borders on blasphemy. Just recently, I had one man in Kansas City stack up hundreds of dollars down on a table asking me to pray a specific prayer of blessing over his business. I refused. Certainly, I could have used this offering for our ministry...it is very needed. But, the spirit and motive behind it reminded me of Acts 8:18-23, "And when Simon saw that through laying on of the apostles' hands the Holy Ghost was given, he offered them money, Saying, Give me also this power, that on whomsoever I lay hands, he may receive the Holy Ghost. But Peter said unto him, Thy money perish with thee, because thou hast thought that the gift of God may be purchased with money. Thou hast neither part nor lot in this matter: for thy heart is not right in the sight of God. Repent therefore of this thy wickedness, and pray God, if perhaps the thought of thine heart may be forgiven thee. For I perceive that thou art in the gall of bitterness, and in the bond of iniquity."

My mind very carefully reviewed all that I could remember about giving offerings to the Lord. Was there an occasion in the Bible where a man specifically gave an offering to the Lord and experienced a direct result? Certainly. "And David built there an altar unto the Lord, and offered burnt offerings and peace offerings. So the Lord was entreated for the land, and the plague was stayed from Israel" (2 Sam. 24:25). This followed the horrible tragedy of 70,000 people dying within 72 hours following David's sin.

Scripturally, the purpose of sowing or giving to God is to create the rewards of obedience.

> ▶ "Honour the Lord with thy substance, and with the firstfruits of all thine increase:" (Prov. 3:9).

▶ "Bring ye all the tithes into the storehouse, that there may be meat in Mine house, and prove Me now herewith, saith the Lord of hosts, if I will not open you the windows of heaven, and pour you out a blessing, that there shall not be room enough to receive it. And I will rebuke the devourer for your sakes, and he shall not destroy the fruits of your ground; neither shall your vine cast her fruit before the time in the field, saith the Lord of hosts. And all nations shall call you blessed: for ye shall be a delightsome land, saith the Lord of hosts" (Mal. 3:10-12).

▶ "Give, and it shall be given unto you; good measure, pressed down, and shaken together, and running over, shall men give into your bosom. For with the same measure that ye mete withal it shall be measured to you again" (Lk. 6:38).

▶ "And Jesus answered and said, Verily I say unto you, There is no man that hath left house, or brethren, or sisters, or father, or mother, or wife, or children, or lands, for My sake, and the gospel's, But he shall receive an hundredfold now in this time, houses, and brethren, and sisters, and mothers, and children, and lands, with persecutions; and in the world to come eternal life" (Mk. 10:29-30).

It astounds me that men who want to believe so many other Scriptures have a problem with these Scriptures. Those who believe what Jesus said about Heaven and hell are incensed that anyone would want to embrace these Scriptures on reward, Harvest and financial response from God to a single act of Seed sowing or an act of disobedience.

Some feel that it is sinful to expect a financial gift from God. Yet, everyday these same individuals beg God for things far more valuable and far more worthy than money. They ask for Wisdom, the salvation of a loved one, the healing of an uncle who has cursed God his entire lifetime. They beg God to send someone to buy their house or car, or even ask the Lord to win a lottery on which they have gambled.

People are peculiar. Maybe even blind.

Anyway, I have got to get back to my story.

I started believing about Jason after I planted the special Seed of $58 and gave it an Assignment— that God would remember my Seed as a testimony of my confidence toward Him regarding His covenant with me.

My money was important to me.

My faith was important to God.

My mind wandered that morning after I planted the Seed. I had gone through a very devastating divorce when my son was just 18 months old. There had been deep difficulties and walls of conflict as his mother had married two more times. Two child custody cases had left me broke. I had really given up any possibility of having my son and being able to raise him in the presence of the Lord in church.

But, I had given my Seed an ASSIGNMENT. You see, a watermelon seed contains an invisible instruction to create watermelons. An apple seed contains an invisible instruction to create apples. A tomato seed never consults a cantaloupe seed with a puzzled question, "What do you think I ought to become?" You see, the Creator of this universe places an instruction...an Assignment...in everything He creates. It may be invisible to the human eye. It may be a silent message or Assignment. But the Harvest reveals what it contains. That's how it is with our Seeds that we sow into this world. It is important to give them invisible instructions and call in the Harvest where we need the results the most.

Within a few weeks, I landed back at the Dallas airport and was very surprised to see my secretary standing there. I could not remember her ever meeting me at the airport before "Jason will be here in one hour at the other airport at Love Field, " she said excitedly.

"What's wrong?" I asked, instantly tense.

"Nothing," she replied. "His mother has just decided that he can come spend the rest of his life with you."

That was the beginning of a most incredible journey of miracles that I have ever known during my whole lifetime.

One night, in a little Bible study in Dallas, I rather hesitatingly told the people about my experiment with the $58 Seed. I suggested that they plant it as a special signal and message to the Lord that they were in covenant with Him for something specific with their life.

"You cannot buy a miracle with money," I insisted as I always do. "But, you can plant this as a Seed of your faith and believe God will provide a supernatural Harvest as He did for my life."

That night a couple wrote the name of their

daughter on their check. She was addicted to cocaine. Her life was in shambles. They were devastated. Fourteen days later, that daughter accepted Christ and was set free from drugs.

It would astound you if I kept every single letter...recorded every single testimonial...perhaps it is best that I have not, though my files are stacked full of incredible letters validating the power of God.

God wants to be worshipped...not His Seed that He provides for us.

Many ministers have asked me about the mystery of the $58 Seed and the covenant with God.

I do not really have any answers. That's like asking Naaman to analyze why dipping seven times in Jordan removed his leprosy. It is like asking Joshua how the marching affected the walls of Jericho so that they fell approximately on the seventh day. It is like asking the blind man to explain the chemistry in the spittle and the clay that removed a lifetime of blindness.

I really do not know. I do speculate a lot. I crave Wisdom. I have an intense appetite to understand what creates currents of miracles.

My thoughts are that it is not the amount of the Seed that matters a whole lot to God. But, whether it is an act of faith. I feel that your Seed is what God multiplies...but your faith is why He multiplies it.

Some have sowed Seed with carnal motives to manipulate, gamble and simply experiment.

I doubt that they will ever see any results to their Seed. God cannot be bought with silver and gold.

Thousands have seen miracles. Unbelievable miracles.

I do believe that any miracle you ever receive from God will require an act of faith on your part. *I also believe that you will have to believe some man of God...somewhere...sometime...before God ever releases a miracle toward you.* "Believe in the Lord your God, so shall ye be established; believe His prophets, so shall ye prosper" (2 Chr. 20:20).

People are cocky these days. Very arrogant toward preachers. They sneer...and the world system will invest millions of dollars to wreck a man's credibility. So, consequently, thousands of naïve and unthinking sheep follow the pied piper of the media over the cliff into the abyss of doubt and unbelief.

Certainly, there are wolves in sheep's clothing. Nobody can doubt that. But, they will stand before their Maker to give an account for every idle word and every false manipulative system and program they have implemented.

14 Important Facts

1.   God wants to bless you in a special way.
2.   God is capable of providing everyone of these 58 kinds of blessings into your life, and into the life of those you love, everyday of your life.
3.   You must do something...some act of obedience before you will experience any rewards for your obedience.
4.   God will often ask you to do something illogical, impractical and something others have never heard of.
5.   God may tell you to do something that He never speaks to others to do...uniquely your personal instruction...because it forces you to use your faith.

6.   What God tells you to do may be for you alone and not others.

7.   God may give an instruction to a man of God who imparts that instruction on to you like He did the widow of Zarephath through Elijah the prophet.

8.   You may have to listen to the prophet's word alone instead of your own inner confirmation of the Spirit. (This happened to the widow of Zarephath. It was the word of the prophet she believed.)

I had an interesting experience in Florida in a conference. A well-known man of God sent me a note, along with other men of God around me, saying he was supposed to address the conference. I never felt it whatsoever. Finally, his tears moved me and I gave him the microphone. The power of God fell through his ministry in an unprecedented way. Miracles happened all over the auditorium. I never felt the presence or the moving of the Holy Spirit during the entire time that he ministered. Even when the service was over, I did not "feel" it whatsoever. God taught me something. He is moving around me whether I feel it or not. Wisdom permits others to honor the Holy Spirit moving within themselves.

9.   If you choose to disobey an instruction of the man of God, you must live with the consequences or losses your doubt has created.

10.   If you are waiting for a specific instruction to come from a man of God that fits with your philosophy, behavior pattern, or the logic of your mind...you may live your entire lifetime without ever experiencing a miracle.

11.   When a man of God gives you an instruction, it is your faith in God that causes the reward system

to work for you.

12.   Your Reaction To A Man Of God Determines God's Reaction To You.

13.   God never tells you to do something that is impossible, but usually illogical.

14.   It is not merely a Seed that you sow (of your time, love, money) but it is your faith that is wrapped around the Seed that really produces the Harvest you desire.

I really hope that when you finish reading this book, that you will sit down and plant a very special Seed of $58 into the work of the Lord somewhere. It certainly does not have to be my own ministry.   I would encourage you to plant it...wrapped with your intense faith in God. Count off fifty-eight days on your calendar.   Then, document the unusual things that begin to happen for good in your life and in the lives of those you love.

You will never be the same again.

Some people will misinterpret this grossly.   It saddens me, but I cannot go another several years without sharing this and giving others access to a potential miracle.

Just a quick closing thought about my mother and father. Financial rivers have never flowed at the Murdock's household. In fact, the highest salary any church ever paid my father as pastor was $125 a week. My father had to pay his own house note, car, etc. Seven children were in our family. Consequently, Mother and Daddy could never afford medical insurance. Especially, they could not begin it while they were in their seventies. Tragedy struck and my mother required a double bypass surgery in Houston,

Texas at a major hospital. Upon leaving the hospital, they found that one of their major bills alone was $48,000 for the surgery. My poor parents scraped every cent they could possibly get together and eventually (with a little help from myself and other children) got the bill to $26,622.

God impressed me to record my story about the $58 Seed on a little cassette tape and send it to my parents and a few other friends. My mother called and said, "Son, Daddy and I felt God on that tape. We're sending a $58 Seed. We sure need some miracles at our house." I knew they did.

It was sort of funny, but my mother called me after one week and said, "Son, it's been a week now and I can't say that I've actually seen any miracles. Am I doing anything wrong?"

I laughed aloud and said, "Of course not, Mother. Give God time."

She did the same thing the following week. But, when I returned home from a meeting at the end of the third week, three messages were on my machine to call home. When my mother and father answered, they were both so excited they could hardly talk.

"Son, I can hardly catch my breath," my father said. He is rarely that talkative. What happened? That hospital had written and called saying, "Your bill of $26,622 came to our attention. Once in a while, we want to do something that helps somebody. Your bill is marked paid in full."

The hospital had paid my mother and father's entire remainder of that specific bill of $26,622.

Coincidence?

Well, what are the chances of it happening to

you? What are the chances of it happening within 21 days from the time you plant a very illogical, impractical and ridiculous Seed of $58? No, I would not build my entire life on a coincidence...not even a one-time experience. My life is built on the Word of the living God. If I never received a Harvest, and I never saw a miracle resulting from any Seed I planted...I would still love my precious Jesus with all my heart, serve God with total abandonment and strive to tell people about Jesus throughout the world. He is what is important on earth, not a few stacks of money.

Please read my heart accurately. I am just saying that at some point in your life..."When You Want Something That You Have Never Had, God Will Tell You To Do Something That You Have Never Done.

That's when *your* Journey of Miracles will finally *begin.*

Something You Have
In Your Hand Can Create
Anything You Want
In Your Future.

-MIKE MURDOCK

～ 5 ～

THOUSANDS ARE UNWILLING TO START THEIR HARVEST WITH A SMALL SEED.

―――――――

Acorns can become oak trees.

But, most people keep waiting for their "ship to come in" before they begin the sowing cycle. You must start *with what you have.*

The Law of Beginning is Powerful. Every long journey starts with the first small step. Millionaires started with their first nickel. Great companies have humble beginnings.

You Can Go Anywhere You Want To Go...If You Are Willing To Take Enough Small Steps.

Look at Mary Kay Ash, the late great legendary businesswoman. She had just a few thousand dollars and a couple of shelves of products. But, she started her business. She focused on her future. At her death, her business was valued at 1.2 billion.

Look at McDonald's hamburger chain. From a humble beginning, it has become the most successful hamburger chain on the earth. It started with a little hamburger that became popular in a town.

If you keep holding on to the Seed you have today, it will never become a Harvest. You must be willing to start your Harvest *with whatever God has already placed in your hand.* I sat in a banquet many years ago frustrated. The speaker stirred me. I desperately wanted to plant a Seed of $1,000 into his ministry. But, I had only $10 in my pocket. "Lord, I really wish I could bless him with a $1,000 check," I whispered to the Lord.

"You have $10 in your pocket. Plant it."

"Oh, I need my $10 tonight. But, if You would give me $1,000, I promise to sow it," was my answer.

My mind started churning. How could I get more money to sow? I thought about my little office. It was in my tiny garage in Houston, Texas. That's where I studied, prayed and also where I had a row of shelves that contained the only product I had in my ministry—one long-play album of music. Five hundred of those albums were on the shelves. That was approximately six to eight months of sales for me. Then it hit me. *"Start with what you already have."*

Little hinges can swing huge doors. I could give him those 500 albums. If he sold them for $6.00 each, he would make $3,000 for his ministry. I made the decision. "Brother, I wish I had a lot to give you. I wanted to be able to write a check for $1,000, but my ministry is just beginning. I do have 500 record albums. If you would receive them from me, you can sell them in your crusades. If you sell them for $1.00 each, it would be a $500 Seed. If you sell them for $6.00, you would have $3,000 for your ministry." (I thought I had to explain this to him!)

Twelve months passed. One day, while sitting in

Nairobi, Kenya, a missionary's home, the mail came. It contained a scribbled hand-written note from a major television minister. "Mike, I heard your record album. I want to purchase 40,000 of them to sell through my television program. Please rush me 40,000 albums. I will send you a check for them next week." I shouted all over that room.

The profit enabled me to purchase a beautiful white Lincoln Town Car...*cash!* It launched an entire different season for my life and ministry. I was on air every time I drove up to a church for a crusade. Why? I started with whatever was already in my hand.

Last week, a lady wrote me a check for $5.00. She was embarrassed. She said, "I'm so ashamed to send you such a small check, but it's all that I have." I was reading her letter about 2:00 in the morning after coming in from a major meeting. My heart was so stirred. You see, what she was planting was *enough to impress God.*

He knows how *much* you have.

He knows how *little* you have.

Your *obedience* always secures His attention.

You don't have to write God a huge check for $100,000 to move His hand toward you. You simply have to obey the inner voice of the Holy Spirit with *whatever you presently possess.*

Remember the incredible scenario of the widow? "And Jesus sat over against the treasury, and beheld how the people cast money into the treasury: and many that were rich cast in much. And there came a certain poor widow, and she threw in two mites, which make a farthing. And He called unto Him His disciples, and saith unto them, Verily I say unto you,

That this poor widow hath cast more in, than all they which have cast into the treasury: For all they did cast in of their abundance; but she of her want did cast in all that she had, even all her living" (Mark 12:41-44).

She started her Harvest with what she had.

I have sowed jewelry, cars and clothes into other lives. I have planted hundreds of thousands of books and tapes as special Seeds. You see, everything you have is a Seed.

If you keep it today, that is your Harvest.

But if you release it, it becomes a Seed.

What you presently possess is only a Seed if you sow it into soil. When you keep it in your hand, it becomes the only Harvest you will ever have. Look around you. Is there a piece of furniture that a widow needs in her house? Could you volunteer two hours a week at your home church? That's a Seed.

Start with what you have.

Are you good at repairing automobiles? Discuss with your pastor your desire to repair the automobile of any widow in your congregation, as a Seed of Love.

You are a Walking Warehouse of Seeds. You have more inside you than you could ever imagine. But, you must take the time to inventory everything God has given you.

Do not permit pride to rob you of an opportunity to plant a Seed. When the offering plate is passed, even if you only possess $2.00 in your pocket—plant it. Get your Harvest started.

As a parent, teach your child the importance of sowing something consistently in the work of God. It may only be a dime or a quarter. But, they will create a flow and river of Harvest that will outlast every attack against their life.

Millions are waiting for more. They refuse to start their Harvest with a small Seed. It is one of the reasons they will never receive everything God wants to send to them. "Though thy beginning was small, yet thy latter end should greatly increase" (Job 8:7).

Our Prayer Together...

"Father, show me the Seeds you have already given to me. I make a decision to sow any Seed you desire regardless of how small it now appears. You will multiply it back where I need it the most today. In Jesus' name. Amen."

You Will Never Change
What You Believe
Until Your Belief System
Cannot Produce Something
You Want.

-MIKE MURDOCK

❧ 6 ❧

MILLIONS ARE NOT EXPERIENCING INCREASE BECAUSE NOBODY HAS YET TOLD THEM ABOUT THE PRINCIPLE OF SEED-FAITH.

The Unlearned Are Simply The Untaught.

Teachers are necessary. You would not have the ability to even read this book, but a teacher entered your life. You sat at their feet. You learned the alphabet. Hour after hour you sat through boring, agitating and often frustrating moments. But, it opened the Golden Door to Life.

You can only know something you have *heard,* something you have been taught. That is why God gives mentors, ministers of the gospel, and parents to impart knowledge. "And He gave some, apostles; and some, prophets; and some, evangelists; and some, pastors and teachers; For the perfecting of the saints, for the work of the ministry, for the edifying of the body of Christ: That we henceforth be no more children, tossed to and fro, and carried about with every wind of doctrine," (Eph. 4:11,12,14).

Everyone understands sowing. Sowing is planting a Seed in soil for a desired Harvest and return.

▶ Seed-faith Is Letting Go Of Something You Have Been Given To Create Something Else You Have Been Promised.

▶ Seed-faith Is Using Something You Have To Create Something Else You Want. When You Let Go Of What Is In Your Hand, God Will Let Go Of What Is In His Hand.

Your Seed is what blesses *another.*

Your Harvest is anything that blesses *you.*

So, Seed-faith is sowing something you possess in faith that God will honor it by bringing a Harvest where you need it the most.

Now, most people have never understood the wonderful, glorious part of this principle of sowing and reaping. In fact, it is usually a threat. You will hear a parent tell a rebellious teenager, "Some day, you're going to reap what you sow!" Now, they rarely say that to the teenager when he is obedient and doing something wonderful! They only emphasize that when they are focusing on something wrong that their child did.

Every minister has used Galatians 6:7 to motivate their congregation to have a healthy fear of God. "Be not deceived; God is not mocked: for whatsoever a man soweth, that shall he also reap." But, if you keep reading after that verse, it is a wonderful and powerful promise that concludes, "...but he that soweth to the Spirit shall of the Spirit reap life everlasting. And let us not be weary in well doing for in due season we shall reap, if we faint not" (Gal. 6:7-9).

The Apostle Paul continues emphasizing this incredible and miraculous principle of Seed-faith. It is his personal encouragement in using this principle to help people do something wonderful for others! "As we have therefore opportunity, let us do good unto all men, especially unto them who are of the household of faith" (Gal. 6:10).

To many, the principle of sowing and reaping in Scripture is a *threat*.

Scripturally, it is a *wonderful and glorious promise* to believers that patience in sowing Seed will produce a Harvest worthy of pursuit.

The principle: You can decide any Harvest you would like to reap and sow a special Seed, wrapped with your faith, for a desired result.

This is Seed-faith.

God works this principle continually. Here is an example: He had a Son, Jesus. But, He wanted a family. So, He planted His best Seed on a place called Calvary to produce a glorious family, the body of Christ. Here we are!

Elijah, the remarkable prophet, understood this principle as much as any other person in Scripture. He looks in the face of an impoverished peasant woman about to eat her last meal. Her son is shriveled and withered, emaciated, laying in the bed. She is destitute. This is not simply a widow seeding more money to make a car note, or pay for her house. Her last piece of bread is the only thing between her and starvation.

But, God has smiled on her. Oh, He did not send her a bag of groceries! (You see, even a bag of groceries would have an end to it.) Elijah did not hand her a $20 bill. That would merely delay starvation of a few more hours.

God sent her a man who understood how to keep creating Harvest after Harvest with a simple Seed. Oh, it is a marvelous day in your life when God sends someone who can see the future of your Seed! You have found favor with angels! You have found favor that will outlast your present trial! You may be staring at your "present" with a total discouragement, but that man of God has a picture of your future.

Elijah did not say, "I will tell the church about your problem and see if anyone can help you." He did not criticize her. He did not ask her if she had been tithing. He pointed to something she already had and told her how to use it as a bridge out of trouble.

▶ Your Seed is the only exit from your present.
▶ Your Seed is the only door into your future.
▶ Your Seed is the bridge of blessing into the world you have dreamed about your entire life.

Elijah did something glorious and wonderful. Something I wish every man of God would do when he stands behind his pulpit and talks to people about an offering for the work of God. He explained that what she already had in her hand contained the solution to her life.

Seed-faith is bringing people beyond the porch of their problem and bringing them into the House of Wisdom, and showing them that every solution to their life is right there in their own hand!

The unconverted can feel empty and hopeless. But, God teaches that the Seed for their salvation is already in their mouth. "But what saith it? The word is nigh thee, even in thy mouth, and in thy heart: that is, the word of faith, which we preach; That if thou shalt confess with thy mouth the Lord Jesus, and shalt believe in thine heart that God hath raised Him from the dead, thou shalt be saved. For with the heart man believeth unto righteousness; and with the mouth confession is made unto salvation" (Rom. 10:8-10).

Think about it! You may be backslidden, broken, tormented and burdened down. Your sins number into the hundreds. Yet, right where you sit this very moment, you can plant a Seed. What is the Seed? Your confession of Christ. In a single moment, millions have moved from a life of emptiness and hopelessness into light and joy. A single Seed of confession can bring a man out of trouble for the rest of his life.

That is Seed-faith. The glorious principle of Seed-faith. Everybody believes in sowing. Few have embraced the promise of the Harvest!

Some have not taught it because they fear criticism. You see, when you begin to talk about money, you are focusing on the core of people's lives. Money is the god of this world. Everything revolves around it. Powerful ministries avoid this topic like the plague. Yet, in the privacy of their leadership sessions, they weep and intercede for God to provide more finances so they can reach this generation.

Some, refusing to discuss the principle of sowing

and reaping often approach the wealthy in the privacy of their homes. There, they request and ask for large donations for their ministry. Through this means, they deflect any criticism that could come from public emphasis.

Some feel that it is unbalanced to talk about money in a church service. Yet, nobody considers a dentist unbalanced because he works only on teeth. Nobody considers a lawyer unbalanced because he only discusses legal matters.

Nobody becomes angry at an evangelist for preaching salvation. Few become furious with a pastor teaching on the principles of loving relationships. Everyone gets excited when thousands receive their healing in a miracle service.

But, the moment money is discussed, another spirit enters the room. The atmosphere changes. The climate is different.

Some do not teach on the principles of prosperity because their own supply is sufficient. Recently, I walked into a million dollar home. It was the residence of a minister friend. He never preaches on financial prosperity. Souls are his focus. He is brilliant at building homes for a profit. He has friends who build a home. Then he moves in. Later, when he sells it, he makes a generous profit. Over the years, he has made a tremendous amount of money. He has no financial problems whatsoever because of his gift of building. He understands contracting, and everything that goes with it.

Many do not have this knowledge and background. So, while he enjoys the beautiful luxury of his million dollar home, thousands sit under his ministry who can hardly make their car payment. Their homes are tiny, cramped and uncomfortable. You see, supply is not his focus any more. So, it has never dawned on him that others have a problem he does not have.

Some do not teach about sowing for a Harvest because of the anger, retaliation and fierce attack that it attracts to their ministry. Nobody who wants to be productive has time for battle. Several years ago, a powerful minister ministered to millions on television. When the media began to set a trap and strategy to destroy him, it cost him millions in lawyer fees. His staff became so fragmented. Their focus was broken. Instead of writing books that helped people, he had to meet with lawyers for hundreds of hours. His tax records were analyzed. Investigators searched through garbage containers to find financial documents and letters from partners.

The ungodly will invest millions to shut the mouth of one man of God. So, many men of God will avoid this teaching so they can retain their focus on people instead of defending their ministry. It's costly. It's devastating, physically and spiritually.

Consequently, their people plunge into poverty and loss because they remain untaught.

Something intrigues me. When the discussion of money and giving to the work of God emerges, the ungodly find a common ground with many religious leaders. They join together—like Pontius Pilate did with the Pharisees of his day for the common goal of crucifying Jesus of Nazareth.

Why is their anger over the message of sowing Seed to create a financial Harvest in your personal life?

Do these people despise giving? I don't think so. You see, our entire earth is a giving earth. Thousands give to the March of Dimes, Muscular Dystrophy telethon, the Red Cross and the Salvation Army. Nobody is angry about your giving—to other people. Their anger involves giving to the work of God.

Are they angry because teaching on prosperity is unnecessary and wasted time? Of course not. Most people do not have enough money to pay their present bills. Most do not even have a car that is paid for. Someone has said 60 percent of Americans would be bankrupt within 90 days if their jobs were stopped or terminated. No, the anger is not because everyone has too much money. Everyone is needy.

Is the anger directed toward all the ministers of the gospel for receiving offerings? I don't believe so. I see many ministers on television who are not criticized when they simply announce that there is a need for an offering so they can build a cathedral. The greatest evangelist of our generation receives offerings in every crusade. He has never been criticized, because his offerings are very low key.

No, the anger is not over receiving offerings. That has gone on for hundreds of years. The anger is not over a church that needs help or widows who need assistance.

Do those who fight the Seed-faith message of prosperity despise money and hate the subject of money? Not at all. I watched a talk show host recently blast his anger fiercely at others who talked about sowing to get prosperity. Yet, he offered his own video at the end of the program for $40. So, he does not hate money. He wants more of it for himself. He is not anti-money. He certainly is not against making a profit.

Those who become infuriated over sowing toward prosperity are angry that a minister promises a hundredfold return from God for their Seed. They hate the teaching that you can "give something you have and get something back in return from God."

The battle is over *Expectation* of a Harvest.

Let's analyze this. Are they angry because they believe God cannot give a Harvest? Most people believe God can do anything.

Do they believe that God should not produce a Harvest from our Seed? I don't think so. Every television reporter searches for impoverished ghetto areas to stir up the consciousness of America toward the poor. Thousands even get angry at God for not doing something for them. Most every human believes God should prosper him.

Do they believe that God will not really prosper people who sow into His work?

Now, there is a lot of controversy over this.

Here is one of the greatest discoveries of my life. The anger over sowing Seed into the work of God to get a Harvest arises because many believe it is wrong to expect something back from God.

The hated word is expectation.

"When I give to God, I expect nothing in return!" bragged one religious leader recently. "I give because I love Him. I give because of obedience. It is greedy to expect something back in return." Yet, this same religious leader expects a paycheck every single week of his life—in return for his spiritual leadership.

It is only expecting money back from God that produces the point of contention.

Is it wrong to give your heart to God and expect forgiveness, mercy and a home in Heaven? Oh, no! That's all right to expect an eternal home in return. Is it wrong to bring your sick body to God and expect Divine healing in return? Few disagree with that.

It is only money that bothers them. Money given to God and His work.

Why is it wrong to expect God to give a hundredfold return? This is not even logical. Think of the hundreds of doctrines taught in the Scriptures. The doctrine of the blood, the Holy Spirit, angels and demons. Think of the horrifying consequences of sin, rebellion and witchcraft. If there should be rebellion to something taught in Scripture, why have we chosen to hate the Principle of Prosperity? It is against every part of our logic to hate something that brings blessing, provision, and ability to bless others.

This is a satanic thing. Oh, my friend, if you could see satan for what he really is, you would despise him with every ounce of your being. He is slimy, slick, and deceptive. He truly is a serpent.

Why isn't there great anger and hatred over the preaching on hell? If I were going to refuse truth, it would be the belief in a hell. You see, it is not even natural to be anti-money.

Suppose you and I were shopping. As we walked through the mall, I saw a man huddled in the corner.

"Oh, there's a man who needs help. He looks hungry. His clothes look tattered. Let's do something good for him." You and I walk over to him.

"Sir, are you all right?"

"No," he mutters. "I have not eaten for four days. I am out of work and unemployed. I am homeless. Can you help me in any way?"

You and I rejoice. Here is our chance to bless this man. "Here, sir. Here is $20. Please buy yourself a good meal at the cafeteria."

Now suppose this happened. He takes the $20 bill. He tears it in pieces. He looks up at us angrily, "Why are you trying to give me a $20 bill?"

You would call this insanity. I would agree. I would say, "Here's a very sick man. He threw away something that could change his pain into pleasure. I handed him an answer, a solution, some money. He acts like it is a trap, a trick, poison."

Yet, the great Provider of this universe hands us the Principle of Prosperity that will rewrite our financial future, and we erupt with anger at the thought that we could sow a Seed and reap a Harvest!

This is insanity!

It is not insanity of the mind; it is insanity of the will, the chosen path of rebellion.

Are we against money? Of course not. When we find a quarter on the pavement, we tell every friend on the telephone that day. When we discover a $20 bill forgotten in the pocket of our old clothes in the corner of the closet, we shout! It brings fresh motivation into us. Maybe it doesn't take a lot to excite us these days —just the unexpected.

The entire warfare over the Seed-faith message and the principles of prosperity is over this— expectation of a financial Harvest back from God.

Now, there is the most incredible truth: *Expectation is the only pleasure man can generate in the heart of God.*

You see, faith is confidence in God.

Expectation Is The Evidence Of Your Faith.

God said that it is impossible to pleasure Him unless you expect something from Him. "But without faith it is impossible to please Him; for he that cometh to God must believe that He is, and that He is a rewarder of them that diligently seek Him" (Heb. 11:6).

You cannot even be saved unless you expect Him to receive you.

You cannot be healed unless you expect Him to heal you.

You cannot be changed unless you expect Him to change you.

God's Only Pleasure Is To Be Believed.

God's Only Pain Is To Be Doubted.

I will say it again, the essence of the entire Bible is Numbers 23:19: "God is not a man, that He should lie; neither the son of man, that He should repent: hath He said, and shall He not do it? Or hath He spoken, and shall He not make it good?"

God is not a man.

Man lies. God does not.

Think about this! God is not pleasured by streets of gold, clouds of angels. He is only happy when somebody is expecting Him to do what He said. What is believing? Expecting God to do something He promised.

This huge controversy is not even about you or your home. Your poverty is not the goal of satan. You are not the real enemy to him.

God is the enemy of satan.

Satan knows what pleasures God—for a human to trust Him, believe Him, depend on Him. Satan remembers the presence of God. He is a former employee.

He is an angel who refused to believe God and is tasting the eternal consequences.

The goal of satan is to rob God of every moment of pleasure received from humans.

How can he rob God? When he stops your expectation of a miracle, he has paralyzed and stopped the only pleasure God experiences. Every time you expect a miracle, you create a river of pleasure through the heart of God. Every time you doubt, you create waves of pain. God has feelings, too.

That is what is behind the anti-prosperity cult on earth.

They are not anti-money.

They are not against your having money.

They are against you expecting any money from God.

Oh, my precious friend, listen to my heart today. Why would men waste time, precious expensive television time, smearing, sneering and destroying other men of God who are praying for people to get out of poverty? This world is impoverished. Somebody said that 40 percent of bankruptcies involve born-again Christians. This world is experiencing a financial crash everyday. You would think that everyone would praise, admire and encourage any man of God who wanted to see them blessed, pay their bills and send their children through college. Why aren't we thanking God aloud and often for the wonderful teaching that our Jehovah is a miracle God of provision?

It is not the teaching that you can have money that is bothering them.

It is the teaching that God will supply you a Harvest when you release your Seed to Him.

When you involve "the expectation of a return" with an offering, you arouse every devil in hell who despises their former boss who is pleasured by our expectation.

They hate the God you love.

They are obsessed with depriving Him of every possible moment of pleasure you are creating in the heart of God.

Your Father simply wants to be believed. That's all. He just wants to be believed. In fact, He promised that if you would just put Him above everything else in your life, He would keep providing anything you needed for the rest of your life (Matt. 6:33). He wants to be believed. He invited you to prove His Word to you (Mal. 3:9-11).

Here is the argument of the anti-prosperity cult. "What about greed? That is materialism. When you expect some money back for giving to God, that is satanic. That is ungodly! That is poisonous and deceptive to offer something back when you give to God."

Then, why did God offer us something back in return for Seed, if that is greed? Do you feel that it is greedy to work for a salary? You are getting something in return!

God anticipated greed. He knew our need and desire for increase could be deceptive, distorted and easily used by satan to manipulate us. So, He built in a "corrective."

He put something in the system of increase that would completely remedy and cure any problem with greed—GIVING.

It is impossible for you to give to God and stay greedy.

That's why He established the tithing system of returning ten percent back to Him.

That's why He promised Peter a hundredfold return for giving up everything to follow Christ (Mk. 10: 28-30).

Every person who sows their Seed has just conquered greed.

Greed hoards.

God gives.

It is impossible to give your way to greed.

Now, inside of each of us is an invisible command to become more, to multiply and increase. The first commandment ever given by God in the Book of Genesis was to multiply and replenish and become more.

God is a God of increase. It is normal to become more, desire more and produce more. Remember the story regarding the man with one talent? He was punished eternally. Why? He did not do anything with his gifts and skills to increase his life. In fact, what he had was given to another person who had multiplied, used his gifts and become productive.

God is not cruel. He is not a liar and deceptive. If He gives you a desire for increase and prosperity, He will place something inside you that can correct the problem it produces. Giving.

All the preaching against greed and materialism

is only necessary for non-tithers and non-givers.

Any discussion with the giver becoming greedy is totally unnecessary. His Seed is proof he has conquered it. His Seed is the corrective to potential greed.

What you can walk away from is something you have mastered. What you cannot walk away from is something that has mastered you.

Weeping will not correct greed.
Screaming will not correct it.

Confession will not stop greed.

Sowing is the only known cure for greed.

Obedience. Just returning the tithe. Just replanting the Seed He puts into your hand.

The entire warfare and controversy over prosperity is to stop God from feelings of pleasure and feeling good about creating humans. You are not the only target. This whole battle does not revolve around you and your family. The controversy is between satan and God. You are only caught in the crossfire.

Your Seed is the only proof you are expecting something in return. The only evidence that a farmer is looking for a Harvest is when you see him sowing his Seed. Your Seed is the only proof you are expecting.

Your words are not the proof. You can talk about many things and still not really be expecting a Harvest.

Now, expectation is only possible when a Seed has been planted.

When you withhold from God, it is impossible for your faith to work and expectation to occur. So, when God speaks to your heart to sow a Seed, you cannot even begin to expect a Harvest until you have obeyed His instruction. Your obedience in sowing immediately positions you to be able to expect.

Sowing does not create expectation.

Sowing authorizes you to expect.

You see, many people sow, but they have not been taught the Principle of Seed-faith—that you should expect something in return. So, millions give to churches and never see a huge return on their Seed. They give to pay the bills of the church. They give because of guilt over withholding after all the blessings they have experienced. They give because a pastor meets with them privately and insists on them making "a donation to the cause." They give for many reasons.

Few really sow their Seed to produce a Harvest.

Few sow with expectation of a real return from God.

How do you know that most do not expect a return? They become angry over sowing. If you believed something was coming back to you a hundred times—you would be more excited in that moment than any other time of your life.

Example: Have you ever received a sweepstakes letter in the mail that you have "won a million dollars?" Of course, you have. Now, when you are young and inexperienced, you get very excited. You tear the envelope open. You can just imagine yourself with a yacht, a beautiful Rolls Royce, and a vacation to Spain. What is happening? Expectation excites you, it energizes you, it creates a flurry of enthusiasm around you.

Expectation.

After you tear the envelope open, you suddenly realize there was a part of the letter you could not see when it was closed. The part that says, "You could be one of those who win a million dollars." After you open the letter, you realize that they did not really promise that you had won it. But, you may have been one of the winners. Your expectation wanes and dies and withers.

You make a telephone call and realize that you were not really one of the winners. Expectation dies. Disappointment sets in.

Any disappointment you are experiencing today reveals your lack of expectation of a Harvest.

So, watch and sense the atmosphere that fills a church when an offering is being received. If there is expectation of a Harvest, joy fills that house.

If expectation is present, joy is present.

Joy Is The Proof Of Expectation.

Depression and disappointment are evidences of the presence of fear. The fear of loss. The fear of less.

Expectation is an impossibility until you sow a Seed.

You can have a need and still not expect an answer.

You can have a great dream and still not expect it to come to pass.

Expectation is produced by obedience.

Obedience is the proof of faith.

Faith is confidence in God.

Peter declared that he had given up everything to follow Christ. What was the reaction of Jesus? Well, He did not commend him for discipleship. He did not commend him for his willingness to suffer. He did not brag on him for being a martyr. Jesus looked at him and promised that he would get everything back that he gave up, one hundred times over (Mk. 10:28-30).

Jesus constantly promoted expectation.

When the woman at the well of Samaria listened to Him, He promised her water that she would never thirst again. When the weary came to Him, He said, "I will give you rest." When the sinful approached Him with humility and confession, He promised them that they were forgiven.

Jesus always responded to those with great expectation. When the blind man cried out and was instructed to be silent by the crowds, Jesus reacted. Many were blind. But one had great expectations of Jesus.

Jesus healed him.

Impossible things happen to those who expect them to happen. "For verily I say unto you, That whosoever shall say unto this mountain, Be thou removed, and be thou cast into the sea; and shall not doubt in his heart, but shall believe that those things which he saith shall come to pass; he shall have whatsoever he saith" (Mk. 11:23).

Anything good is going to find you.

Anything from God is going to search you out.

Anything excellent is going to become obvious to you.

That's the principle of Seed-faith.

You have been given something by God that has a future. When you discover your Seed, wrap your faith around it with great expectation. This will empower you to produce the financial Harvest you have desired for your lifetime.

Your Seed Is The Only
Influence You Have
Over Your Future.

-MIKE MURDOCK

❧ 7 ❧

MOST PEOPLE HAVE NEVER LEARNED THE SECRET OF GIVING THEIR SEED A SPECIFIC ASSIGNMENT.

Every Seed Contains An Invisible Instruction.

Let me explain. You cannot see it. It is too small and invisible to the natural eye. But, it is obviously there. If you could look deep into the watermelon seed, you would see an invisible instruction to "produce a watermelon." Tomato seeds contain invisible instructions to "produce tomatoes."

There is no wavering or uncertainty. It is precise, exact and specific. The Creator had decided the Harvest when He created the Seed.

When God wanted a family, He sowed His Son. He gave His Son an Assignment to "seek and save that which was lost." Jesus was the best Seed God ever planted on earth. But, He contained an assignment, an instruction, a purpose. Everything He did was connected to that Assignment every day of His life.

David tapped into this incredible secret of giving his Seed a specific Assignment. When thousands lay dead across the city, he cried out to God and brought Him a specific offering for a specific purpose. "And David built there an altar unto the Lord, and offered burnt offerings and peace offerings. So the Lord was entreated for the land, and the plague was stayed from Israel" (2 Sam. 24:25).

Elijah taught this incredible Principle of Assignment to the widow of Zarephath. As she was going to bring water, he gave her a specific instruction..."Bring me, I pray thee, a morsel of bread in thine hand."

Then, he did something few ministers ever do. He gave her a photograph of what her Seed was going to produce. "For thus saith the Lord God of Israel, The barrel of meal shall not waste, neither shall the cruse of oil fail, until the day that the Lord sendeth rain upon the earth" (1 Kings 17:14).

When you give your Seed an Assignment, incredible faith pours into you. You can see beyond the sacrifice of the moment. The widow did. "And she went and did according to the saying of Elijah: and she, and he, and her house, did eat many days" (1 Kings 17:15).

Does it really work? If you sow for a specific reason, toward a Harvest, does it work? It works if you are doing it in total obedience to the instructions of God. "And the barrel of meal wasted not, neither did the cruse of oil fail, according to the word of the Lord, which he spake by Elijah" (1 Kings 17:16). Those instructions may be through a servant of God, the Word of God or through the inner voice of the Holy

Spirit.

Your prayers are Seeds, too.

Job sowed a prayer of deliverance for his three friends. What happened? God turned Job's captivity around! Just like David had stopped a tragedy by offering a special offering to the Lord.

Many years ago, I experienced a personal attack. It was devastating to me emotionally. My mind was fragmented. Inside my heart was broken, and I wanted to die. It was a situation that would have been complicated by any retaliation or attempts of explanation. I flew to Los Angeles for another crusade on the same day. The next morning, a Sunday, the Holy Spirit gave me a strange instruction. "Plant a battle Seed."

I had never heard of such a thing. *When You Want Something You Have Never Had, You Have Got To Do Something You Have Never Done.*

Then, I remembered when David had aimed his Seed like an arrow. He gave it an Assignment. He focused it for a desired result. And the plague was stayed (2 Sam. 24:25).

I planted everything I had that day—$3,000. Supernaturally the attack ended as suddenly as it had began. Isn't that wonderful? You always have a Seed that becomes an exit from your present circumstances.

Your Seed Is Always The Door Out Of Trouble. It is anything you do that helps another person. Your Seed is anything that improves the life of someone near you. It may be the Seed of information, Seed of encouragement or even the Seed of finances. Whatever you want, you must remember to give your

Seed a specific Assignment so that your faith will not waver. "But let him ask in faith, nothing wavering. For he that wavereth is like a wave of the sea driven with the wind and tossed. For let not that man think that he shall receive any thing of the Lord. A double minded man is unstable in all his ways" (James 1:6-8). Your faith must have a specific instruction. Not two. Not three. One. "This one thing I do," were the words of the great man of God. David cried out, "My heart is fixed" (Ps. 57:7).

Don't waver. Aim your Seed. "Turn not to the right hand or to the left, that thou mayest prosper whithersoever thou goest" (Josh. 1:7).

Giving your Seed a specific Assignment strongly impacts your focus. And focus matters. The secret of success is concentration. The Only Reason Men Fail Is Broken Focus.

It is a tragic situation that I have observed on many Sunday mornings in churches. The offering is being received. The pastor explains how the offering will be spent, "We really need a roof. This present roof is in need of repair. Will you help us today?"

The people respond. But their Seed has not really received an instruction. Of course it pays the bills. But, it does not really multiply back into their lives. Why? It has not been aimed to create a specific Harvest or desired result. You see, if the only desired result involved is to pay the roofer, that is accomplished easily...but the Seed sowers never receive their personal Harvest in return.

Sow your Seed *consistently.* Generously. And *always in obedience* to the voice of God. Then, wrap your faith around your Seed and target it like an arrow. Enter into a covenant for a specific and desired result in your life.

Thousands fail to do this and never enjoy the financial Harvest God promised. "...ye have not, because ye ask not" (James 4:2).

Our Prayer Together:

"Father, you gave Jesus, your best Seed, an Assignment. You wanted a Family. Now, millions are born again and changed forever. You are producing the Harvest you desired. Teach us the Principle of Assignment—giving every Seed we sow a specific Assignment. Remind us to water and nurture this Seed with expectation, doubting nothing. In Jesus' name. Amen."

Seed-Faith Is Sowing What
You Have Been Given...
To Create What You Have
Been Promised.

-MIKE MURDOCK

⮌ 8 ⮎

MANY HAVE NEVER BEEN TAUGHT TO SOW WITH AN EXPECTATION OF A RETURN.

You Can Only Do What You Know.

Thousands have been taught that it is wrong to expect something in return when you give to God.

They feel that this is proof of greed.

"When I give to God, I expect nothing in return!" is a prideful claim of many who have been trapped by tragic and erroneous teaching.

Do you expect a salary from your boss at the end of the week? Of course, you do. Is this greed? Hardly. Did you expect forgiveness when you confessed your sins to Christ? Of course, you did. Is this greed? Hardly.

Stripping expectation from your Seed is theft of the only pleasure God knows.

Remember, His greatest pleasure is to be believed. His greatest pain is to be doubted. "But without faith it is impossible to please Him: for He that cometh to God must believe that He is, and that He is a rewarder of them that diligently seek Him" (Heb. 11:6).

Motive means your reason for doing something.

When someone is on trial accused of murder, prosecutors try to find the possible motive or reason why he should have been motivated to do such a horrible thing.

God expected you to be motivated by supply, the promise of provision. "Give, and it shall be given unto you; good measure, pressed down, and shaken together, and running over, shall men give into your bosom. For with the same measure that ye mete withal it shall be measured to you again" (Lk. 6:38). (This is much more than a principle of mercy and forgiveness. This is a Principle of Supply.)

God offers overflow as a reason you should sow Seed! Seeds of forgiveness or whatever you need. "Honour the Lord with thy substance, and with the firstfruits of all thine increase: So shall thy barns be filled with plenty, and thy presses shall burst out with new wine" (Prov. 3:9-10). Notice that God paints the picture of overflowing barns to motivate us (give us a reason) for honoring Him.

God promised benefits to those who might be fearful about tithing. "Bring ye all the tithes into the storehouse, that there may be meat in Mine house, and prove Me now herewith, saith the Lord of hosts, if I will not open you the windows of heaven, and pour you out a blessing, that there shall not be room enough to receive it" (Mal. 3:10).

Read Deuteronomy 28:1-14. Here in the Scripture, God creates a list of the specific blessings that will occur if you obey Him. Why does He give us these Portraits of Prosperity?

Peter needed this kind of encouragement just like

you and I do today. He felt such emptiness as he related to Christ that he and the others had "given up everything."

Jesus promised him a one hundredfold return.

"Then Peter began to say unto him, Lo, we have left all, and have followed Thee. And Jesus answered and said, Verily I say unto you, There is no man that hath left house, or brethren, or sisters, or father, or mother, or wife, or children, or lands, for My sake, and the gospel's, But he shall receive an hundredfold now in this time, houses, and brethren, and sisters, and mothers, and children, and lands, with persecutions; and in the world to come eternal life" (Mk. 10:28-30).

Many people think this is evil to sow for a Harvest. That is the reason to sow!

Giving is the cure for greed, not hoarding.

When you sow to get a Harvest, you have just mastered greed.

Greed hoards.

Man withholds.

Satan steals.

The nature of God alone is the giving nature. When you give, you have just revealed the nature of God is inside you.

The only pleasure God receives is through acts of faith. I stress this again. His only need is to be believed. His greatest need is to be believed. "God is not a man, that he should lie" (Num. 23:19).

If an unbeliever confesses to a pastor after church, "I want to give my heart to Christ, pastor." The pastor prays. Suppose the unbeliever then says, "Will you pray that God will give me peace and forgiveness for my confession?"

Imagine a pastor who would reply with indignation—"Of course not! That's greedy. You want something back for giving your heart to Christ?" You would be shocked if your pastor said this.

Your Father offers Supply for Seed; forgiveness for confession; order for chaos.

When Jesus talked to the woman at the well of Samaria, He promised her water that she would never thirst again. Was He wrong to offer her something if she pursued Him? Of course not. That was the purpose of the portrait of water—to motivate her and give her a reason for obeying Him.

One day, my dear friend Dwight Thompson, the powerful evangelist, told me a story about the papaya. If that was consistent, one papaya seed will produce a plant containing ten papayas. If each of the ten papayas contained 470 seeds, there would be 4,700 papaya seeds on one plant.

Now, just suppose you replant those 4,700 seeds to create 4,700 more plants. Do you know how much 5,000 plants containing 5,000 seeds would be? Twenty five million seeds...on the second planting alone.

And we are having trouble really believing in the hundredfold return. Why?

Millions must unlearn the poisonous and traitorous teaching that it is wrong to expect anything in return.

Expectation is the powerful current that makes the Seed work for you. "But without faith it is impossible to please Him: for he that cometh to God must believe that He is, and that He is a rewarder of them that diligently seek Him" (Heb. 11:6).

Expect protection as God promised. "And I will

rebuke the devourer for your sakes, and he shall not destroy the fruits of your ground; neither shall your vine cast her fruit before the time in the field, saith the Lord of hosts" (Mal. 3:11).

Expect favor from a Boaz close to you. "Give, and it shall be given unto you; good measure, pressed down, and shaken together, and running over, shall men give into your bosom. For with the same measure that ye mete withal it shall be measured to you again" (Lk. 6:38).

Expect financial ideas and Wisdom from God as a Harvest. "But thou shalt remember the Lord thy God: for it is He that giveth thee power to get wealth, that He may establish His covenant which He sware unto thy fathers, as it is this day" (Deut. 8:18).

Expect your enemies to fragment and be confused and flee from you. "The Lord shall cause thine enemies that rise up against thee to be smitten before thy face: they shall come out against thee one way, and flee before thee seven ways" (Deut. 28:7).

Expect God to bless you for every act of obedience. "And it shall come to pass, if thou shalt hearken diligently unto the voice of the Lord thy God, to observe and to do all His commandments which I command thee this day, that the Lord thy God will set thee on high above all nations of the earth: And all these blessings shall come on thee, and overtake thee, if thou shalt hearken unto the voice of the Lord thy God" (Deut. 28:1-2).

A businessman approached me, "I don't believe Jesus meant what He said about the hundredfold. We've misunderstood that."

"So, you intend to teach Jesus how to talk when

you get to heaven?" I laughed.

If He will do it for a papaya...He will do it for you and me. We are His children, not merely fruit on a tree!

I believe one of the major reasons people do not experience a supernatural abundant Harvest in finances is because they really do not expect Jesus to do what He said He would do.

Low expectations disappoint God.

When you sow with expectation, your "Seed" will stand before God as a testimony of your faith and confidences.

▶ Sow expecting God to respond favorably to every act of confidence in Him.

▶ Sow from every paycheck.

▶ Sow expectantly, generously and faithfully.

When you start looking and expecting God to fulfill His promise, the Harvest you have needed so long will come more quickly and bountifully than you have ever dreamed.

Our Prayer Together...

"Father, teach us the Wonder of Expectation. Show us how it pleasures You to be believed. Hasten the Harvest as we depend on Your incredible integrity. In Jesus' name. Amen."

≈ 9 ≈

MILLIONS REFUSE TO OBEY THE VERY BASIC AND SIMPLE LAWS OF GOD.

———————➤◆◄———————

Disobedience Produces Losses.

The Scriptures warn, "If ye be willing and obedient, ye shall eat the good of the land: But if ye refuse and rebel, ye shall be devoured with the sword: for the mouth of the Lord hath spoken it" (Isa. 1:19-20).

You can argue about it.

You can rebel against it.

You can complain about it.

But, you cannot read the Scriptures without understanding clearly that obedience produces the river of blessing while disobedience brings famine and desolation.

"Oh, I know some wealthy people who do not serve God at all. They do not attend church, and they do not read the Scriptures. So, why are they prospering?" Good question. And, quite easy to answer, too.

They are probably obeying the basic principles of

prosperity established in Scripture.

Let's look at some of these basic principles and laws that are established quite clearly in Scripture. God said, "And it shall come to pass, if thou shalt hearken diligently unto the voice of the Lord thy God, to observe and to do all His commandments which I command thee this day, that the Lord thy God will set thee on high above all nations of the earth: And all these blessings shall come on thee, and overtake thee, if thou shalt hearken unto the voice of the Lord thy God" (Deut. 28:1-2).

1. *The Principle Of Work.* God only promised to bless the work of your hands. "The Lord shall open unto thee his good treasure, the heaven to give the rain unto thy land in his season, and to bless all the work of thine hand: and thou shalt lend unto many nations, and thou shalt not borrow" (Deut. 28:12).

It is not an option. It is not merely a good "idea" to work everyday. The Apostle Paul wrote that those who refuse to be productive should be denied food. "For even when we were with you, this we commanded you, that if any would not work, neither should he eat" (2 Thess. 3:10).

Those who refuse to work are called disorderly and busybodies in other people's business. "For we hear that there are some which walk among you disorderly, working not at all, but are busybodies" (2 Thess. 3:11).

You must withdraw and withhold any friendship, and time of fellowship, with those rebellious toward working. "And if any man obey not our word by this epistle, note that man, and have no company with him, that he may be ashamed" (2 Thess. 3:14). Note that man. In other words, draw attention to that man. Everyone should mark the lazy person.

"But, I lost my good job. I am waiting for one better to come along," one girl complained.

The principle of work simply reveals the need to be productive. Joseph was productive. He was not in the perfect place, the prison, when he received his promotion. But, he produced and solved problems wherever God placed him. As I told a young man working for me one day, "Son, you may not enjoy what you are doing here in this ministry right now. But, if you don't become productive and complete the instructions I am already giving you, the next season will not be a step up. God will make you run the same lap over and over and over again until you learn this principle.

2. *The Principle Of Diligence.* Diligence means speedy attention to an assigned task. "He becometh poor that dealeth with a slack hand: but the hand of the diligent maketh rich." Laziness is one of the many reasons people do not experience financial Harvest. "He that sleepeth in Harvest is a son that causeth shame" (Prov. 10:4-5).

Diligent people become supervisors and leaders. "The hand of the diligent shall bear rule: but the slothful shall be under tribute" (Prov. 12:24).

The diligent will always have plenty. "The soul of the sluggard desireth, and hath nothing: but the soul of the diligent shall be made fat" (Prov. 13:4).

Those who are diligent become creative in discovering new ways to solve problems. "The thoughts of the diligent tend only to plenteousness; but of every one that is hasty only to want" (Prov. 21:5).

Leaders pursue the company and presence of diligent workers. "Seest thou a man diligent in his business? he shall stand before kings; he shall not stand before mean men" (Prov. 22:29).

The diligent continuously evaluate the results of their efforts. "Be thou diligent to know the state of thy flocks, and look well to thy herds" (Prov. 27:23).

Find the problem closest to you and solve it.

Ask others how to bear the burdens they are presently bearing. Listen carefully to things that bring strife to your boss. Solve them.

► Review your master list of tasks and complete them one by one every single day.

► Labor for compilations instead of allowing a project to run on and on.

► Pursue correction from the one who signs your paycheck.

► Accept rebuke with thankfulness instead of retaliation and resentment.

► Flourish where you are presently working and the news will travel.

3. *The Principle Of Wisdom.* When you increase Wisdom, you will increase your wealth. "Counsel is Mine, and sound Wisdom: I am understanding; I have strength. By Me kings reign, and princes decree justice. By Me princes rule, and nobles, even all the judges of the earth. I love them that love Me; and those that seek Me early shall find Me. Riches and honour are with Me; yea, durable riches and right-eousness. My fruit is better than gold, yea, than fine gold; and My revenue than choice silver. I lead in the way of righteousness, in the midst of the paths of

judgment: That I may cause those that love Me to inherit substance; and I will fill their treasures" (Prov. 8:14-21).

You must become good at what you do.

Study, attend seminars and be mentored. "Wise men lay up knowledge:" (Prov. 10:14).

Prosperous people are usually knowledgeable people. "For the merchandise of it is better than the merchandise of silver, and the gain thereof than fine gold. Length of days is in her right hand; and in her left hand riches and honour" (Prov. 3:14,16). They may not know everything about everything—but they are skilled and developed in at least one topic of their chosen pursuit. You must find the gifts and skills already planted within you.

What you love is a clue to the Wisdom you pursue. If you love computers, that is a clue that you will have special Wisdom in that area. If you have a love for children, you will have a Wisdom toward children.

► When you find what you love, you will find your Wisdom.

► When you find your Wisdom, you will be paid to solve problems with it.

4. *The Principle Of Waiting.* Nobody wants to wait for anything. Sam Walton, the late billionaire, once said that he never invested in a company for where it would be within 18 months. He examined carefully to see where the company would arrive within ten years or longer. Some Japanese businessmen have 100-year goals. A friend of mine once told me that if my father had put $100 a month in a special money market account, I would have been

a multimillionaire in my twentieth birthday.

"Then, why isn't everyone a millionaire if $100 a month put aside for 20 years could create such wealth?" I asked.

"Nobody wants to wait 20 years to spend their $100," was his reply.

What is the proof that people will not wait? When they receive a raise on their job, they immediately make a purchase to obligate that raise. Instead of living within the boundaries of their lower budget and placing the money in a special investment, they make a purchase that produces a pleasure instead of a future.

5. *The Principle Of Mentorship.* You must be teachable. You must have a mentor. Your mentor must be someone qualified to impart knowledge for your life in the arena of finances. You can have a spiritual mentor who is marvelous in prayer and yet unlearned in finances. You can have someone who wants to teach you their opinions, but who does not have any financial success to substantiate and support their teaching.

Who are you pursuing? What are the last three financial questions you have asked? To whom did you ask these questions? What have you done about their answers? What investment opportunities are you ignoring? Pursuing? Considering?

Recently, I felt impressed to get involved in a small financial opportunity. It would require hardly any time. But, I had faith in the head of the company. I shared it with several close to me. I even offered to help make the investment. Some embraced it immediately. Why? They trusted their instincts, my judgment, and the plan presented. Others never even showed up for the second meeting. Yet, they will complain in the coming years of their life how their financial life has been stressful, difficult and almost intolerable. But, they totally refused my mentorship regarding their finances.

"But, I've asked everyone to help me learn how to handle my finances," wailed one young lady.

"What do you want them to teach you?" I asked.

So, I took two or three hours and carefully walked her through her checkbook. I emphasized the importance of maintaining balance awareness— knowing at all times how much money is in your account. I emphasized to her the importance of keeping a small amount of cash with her at all times. She did neither. If you refuse to follow the first two instructions of a mentor, do you qualify for a repeat visit?

"How many have been to a certified financial planner within the last three years?" I asked a large audience one day. Three hands went up.

► Everyone wants a miracle instead of mentorship.

► Quality mentorship is often the biggest miracle you need.

Nobody can force you to pursue knowledge. Usually it takes a tragedy to produce a desire for mentorship.

6. *The Principle Of Integrity.* Integrity is simply doing what you say you will do for someone. Integrity is being what you tell everybody you are.

Integrity is truthfulness.

"If you will give me $40, I will process these four pieces of excess luggage through the airlines," said a skycap to me one day when I was at the airport. The excess was going to cost me over $200. He wanted a generous tip to do it. I always tip generously, but God had been dealing with me strongly about integrity, honesty and doing everything the right way. You see, if nobody on earth is watching, the Boss of the universe is always still watching. "For the eyes of the Lord run to and fro throughout the whole earth, to shew Himself strong in the behalf of them whose heart is perfect toward Him. Herein thou hast done foolishly: therefore from henceforth thou shalt have wars" (2 Chr. 16:9).

"Why don't we just do the right thing?" I countered.

"Sir, it will cost you over $200," he was exasperated with me.

"I know. But, I would rather pay the excess now and feel my conscious at peace than to simply give you a large tip and save the excess luggage fee."

Thousands paid their expense account every week. Some add tips in their expense report that really did not exist or take place. Many will take extra time off for lunch and have someone use the punch-out clock for them. Many employees have taken pencils, pens, legal pads, notebooks and other supplies home to their children and family.

God sees it all. The Principle of Integrity will stand when every excuse falls apart.

Quality is a part of integrity. Show me any person who does poor work, and I'll show you a person without integrity. If you do a sloppy job of painting the house for somebody, put a used part in an automobile engine and charge for a new one, you will eventually lose your business. Customers talk. Truth emerges. Integrity will stand the test of time, criticism wand even mistakes.

Those who will lie will steal also.

You see, lying is simply theft of the truth. Truth is so important. It is the only ingredient that enables us to make quality decisions. So, if someone withholds from you important truths, they have stolen from you the only ingredient you can have to make a good decision. If someone lies to you, lock your cabinets, your doors and keep them away from your life. Even if they are relatives. The laws of God are too important to ignore.

Thousands will never walk the path to plenty because they have totally disregarded the integrity and infallibility of the Holy Scriptures and the Basic Principles of Prosperity.

7. *The Principle Of Respect.* The second Law of Prosperity is to honor your parents (Ex. 20:12). Your Reaction To Your Parents Determines God's Reaction To You.

The Holy Spirit shows your parents it was His first decision concerning your life. Honoring that decision guarantees Divine Provision.

Modern prosperity teaching should include this Law of Honor. It is the hidden mystery to unleashing financial favor on earth.

The Seasons Of Your Life
Will Change Every Time You
Decide To Use Your Faith.

-MIKE MURDOCK

❧ 10 ❧

MILLIONS DO NOT INSTANTLY OBEY THE HOLY SPIRIT WITHOUT NEGOTIATION.

The Holy Spirit Will Not Argue With You.

He is the gift of the Father to those who obey Him. He will woo you. He will tug on your heart. He is gentle, kind and long-suffering.

But, He will not enter into a debate with you. He despises strife, confusion and struggle. "And the servant of the Lord must not strive; but be gentle unto all men," (2 Tim. 2:24).

He will move away from our attacks and quarrelsome spirit. "But foolish and unlearned questions avoid, knowing that they do gender strifes" (2 Tim. 2:23).

Do not argue with the Source of your supply. Stop looking for reasons to avoid sowing. Honor His integrity. He is not unfair. He is not unjust. When He whispers to your heart to take a step of faith, leap forward. Run toward your Harvest.

"Well, I don't want to simply plant out of an emotional feeling!" one minister friend of mine explained.

"Everything you do is emotional," I replied. "When you drag a moment of faith through the sewage of logic, you destroy its impact and influence. Be swift to obey His voice."

I experienced an unusual miracle in my life when I was about 23 years old. I had been on the evangelistic field two or three years. My first year as an evangelist brought me $2,263 income. (One month my entire income was $35. Another month it was $90. I lived in a house that my father had purchased for $150. The entire house!)

Eventually, I had enough money saved to buy a suit and some clothes. It had taken a good while, but I finally saved up $200. I had two $100 bills inside my wallet. I was rather proud but thankful for it. I felt secure. I was anxious to get to a store to buy some clothes.

A young evangelist friend of mine was preaching in a local church. So, I decided to hear him. While he was speaking, I felt the inner tug of the Holy Spirit to plant the $200 into his ministry. I explained to the Lord that my plans were to purchase clothes, so I could look good for His work. The longer he ministered, the more miserable I felt. A heaviness was in me. I thought of every reason to keep the $200. Inside, I began to negotiate with the Holy Spirit. I really did not have a desire to plant any Seed whatsoever. But, I knew His voice.

Somewhere, during some service of a man of God, the Holy Spirit is going to raise your level of desire to please Him. You may not have a lot of joy during the sowing. You may even experience inner conflict and mind confusion, but something in you will become so strong and intense that your desire to please Him will overwhelm your logic, your fears and your greed. It is that miracle moment when your desire to obey Him becomes so powerful that you open the windows of Heaven toward your life.

After the service, I went to him and handed him the $200. He was thrilled. I was rather saddened, but tried to hide it. It was my clothes money.

Seven days later, I was laying in bed at midnight. The telephone rang.

"Brother Mike Murdock?"

"Yes."

"You don't really know me. My husband and I were in your services a year ago here in Memphis. My son died four weeks ago, and God told my husband and me to start treating you like our boy. God told us to buy you some clothes. Are you coming through Memphis any time soon?" What do you think! I didn't care if I had to go through Australia and Russia to get to Memphis, I was going to arrive in Memphis...very soon.

When I got off the plane, she took me to the nicest men's store in Memphis, Tennessee. She bought me four suits, shirts and shoes. Six months later, they did it again. Six months later, they did it again. Six months later, they did it again. And again. Again. And again.

Later, I went to hear a friend of mine in Houston at his church on a Sunday night. Halfway through his sermon, he stopped. He pointed back to me on the back row and said, "It is so good to have Mike Murdock here tonight. The Holy Spirit just spoke to me to stop the service and receive him an offering to buy him some clothes." I was stunned.

On a Wednesday night, I drove across town to another church. I had never met this pastor before. Halfway through his Bible study, he looked back and noticed me on the back seat.

"I see Mike Murdock here tonight. Brother, you and I have never met before, but I have seen you in various conferences. It is wonderful to have you. The Holy Spirit just spoke to my heart to stop the service and receive you an offering to buy you some clothes.

I was in Louisville, Kentucky, and my pastor friend said, "What are you doing tomorrow morning?"

"What do you want to do?" I replied.

"The Holy Spirit spoke to my heart to buy you some clothes," he replied.

I was sitting next to a minister friend of mine in Illinois. He leans over to me and whispers in church, "When are you leaving tomorrow?"

"Why?" I asked.

"I felt the Lord wanted me to buy you a Breoni suit tomorrow." (The next day he purchased it for me. Though he got it wholesale, the retail price on it was $3,220!)

One of my closest friends, Nancy Harmon, called me to her house. I walked in and there were clothes from one end of the room to the other. "The Lord told me to buy you some clothes," she said.

You see, I had walked away from my clothes money. Now, God was supernaturally talking to people about replacing my clothes money by purchasing clothes for me.

What You Are Willing To Walk Away From

Determines What God Will Bring To You.

Please, never argue with the Source of every miracle you desire. When God Talks To You About A Seed, He Has A Harvest On His Mind. You see, He knew the future He was planning. So He gave me faith to plant the Seed that would create my desired future. He gave me the desire, the Seed and the soil where it would grow the quickest.

You can grieve the Holy Spirit through debating.

You can cause Him to withdraw from you when you negotiate and move away from faith.

Faith attracts Him. Faith excites Him. Expectation is His pleasure. Do not rob Him of that moment of obedience.

Delayed obedience can become disobedience.

Millions have lost a thousand Harvests because they became intellectual, negative and argumentative when the Holy Spirit began to whisper an instruction to their heart.

I was in Jacksonville, Florida, a few days ago. The secretary of the pastor came to me weeping. Her husband was by her side.

"Here is the best Seed God has told us to sow. Please take it." It was her wedding rings, the most precious treasure she had. (When you plant a Seed that you can feel, God will feel it, too. You must plant something significant to you before it becomes significant to God.)

That was Monday night.

Five days later, Friday night, she stood at a special School of the Holy Spirit with incredible joy on her countenance and gave her testimony. Somebody who knew nothing of her sacrificial Seed of her rings had decided to bless her. They became a Boaz to her. They gave her a ring worth 100 times the cost of her own rings.

"Then Peter began to say unto Him, Lo, we have left all, and have followed Thee. And Jesus answered and said, Verily I say unto you, There is no man that hath left house, or brethren, or sisters, or father, or mother, or wife, or children, or lands, for My sake, and the gospel's, But he shall receive an hundredfold now in this time, houses, and brethren, and sisters, and mothers, and children, and lands, with persecutions; and in the world to come eternal life" (Mk. 10:28-30).

God is not a man that He should lie.

He wants to be believed.

Nobody can use your faith for you.

Nobody can dream bigger for you.

Nobody can plant the Seed for you.

Nobody. Not your mother, father, or boss, or child.

Every man will give an account of himself to God.

Sometimes, I picture this scenario. Everybody is approaching the Throne of Accountability. They want answers to questions. They want God to explain why they were poor. He will ask the same question.

"Why where you poor when I promised you one hundredfold return for everything you would plant in My work? I told you if you would obey My principles, be diligent and expect Me to do what I promised, I would open the windows of heaven and pour you out a blessing that you could not contain. I, too, want to know why you decided to disregard my instructions and remain without the financial harvest."

That might be the Weeping Night of Eternity when everybody recognizes that the principles were accessible, available and usable—just ignored.

Now, you can begin your journey to prosperity. Be willing to take it a step at a time. Do not rush it. Be careful to obey His voice. Review this book carefully. Bring it with you into the Secret Place of prayer. Talk to the Holy Spirit and ask Him every single step you should take at this time. Bring your stack of bills and credit cards and place them on top of this book. Anoint them, and invite the supernatural intervention of God to break the financial poverty and spirit of lack that has affected and influenced your life.

Ask Him to give you a hatred of poverty and a love and desire for supernatural provision. Discuss your dreams and financial goals in detail with Him. Believe that He will send a Boaz into your life to bless you in many ways.

When He talks to your heart about planting a Seed into His work, do not hesitate. Do not negotiate. And, do not manipulate. The Holy Spirit honors integrity where He finds it.

Confess any sin. Admit if you have withheld the tithes and the offerings He asked. Repent with humility, integrity and expectation of a change in your life. You will see the changes come sooner than you dreamed. *TODAY IS THE POOREST YOU WILL EVER BE THE REST OF YOUR LIFE.*

Our Prayer Together...

"Father, I have opened my heart and received this Seed of Revelation that can change my life forever. Now, use this Seed to grow an Uncommon Harvest. Oh, bless the obedient, the willing and the hungry. In Jesus' name. Amen."

The Greatest Quality On
Earth Is The Willingness
To Become.

-MIKE MURDOCK

❧ 11 ❧

SOME REBEL AGAINST AN INSTRUCTION FROM A FINANCIAL DELIVERER GOD HAS ANOINTED TO UNLOCK THEIR FAITH DURING THEIR TIME OF CRISIS.

━━━━◦━◦━

You Are Not Forgotten By God. *Ever.*

Nobody loves you more than the Person Who created you. Your fears are known by Him. Your tears matter to Him. When you are hurting, He is bringing answers toward you. Every moment of your life, God schedules miracles like currents of blessing into your life.

Every Future Has A Door.

Every River Has A Bridge.

Every Mountain Has A Tunnel.

But, you must find it. Look for it. Listen for it. Search for it. Believe that it exists. "There hath no temptation taken you but such as is common to man:

but God is faithful, Who will not suffer you to be tempted above that ye are able; but will with the temptation also make a way to escape, that ye may be able to bear it" (1 Cor. 10:13).

You must pursue those God is using to fuel your faith. There are wonderful men and women of God who carry financial anointings. They can unlock your faith. It may involve a four-hour drive to their crusade. But, it is very important that you honor and treasure and pursue their mantle. Listen to their tapes. Read their books. Listen to their heart.

They have tasted failure. They know how to get out of trouble. They know what sleepless nights are like. They have fought the demons of fear and uncertainty.

That's why they are qualified to mentor you.

Some will never taste their financial Harvest because they are sitting under leaders who fuel their doubts and unbelief. They listen to relatives who continuously discuss the economic problems on the earth, hard times and how difficult life is.

The voices you keep listening to are the voices you will eventually believe.

Ten spies infected millions of the Israelites with their unbelief and doubt. When they talked about the giants, the people forgot about the grapes of blessing.

What you talk about increases.

What you think about becomes larger.

Your mind and your mouth are magnifiers of anything you want to grow.

Two spies came back with faith, victory and the ability to overcome giants. Their names were Joshua and Caleb. They had been with God. They had seen the giants, but were not afraid. They had seen the grapes and decided to become champions. They had experienced too many days in the wilderness to be satisfied with failure.

They became the champions of faith. Joshua became the leader after the death of Moses. Caleb became known for "taking his mountain." Oh, the rewards of faith are sweet. The taste of victory stays in your mouth so long!

You must discern the Joshuas and Calebs around you. Find the faith-food. Listen for faith-talk. Sit under it and listen and absorb. Something within you will grow.

I receive much inspiration from the story of Elijah and the widow in 1 Kings 17. I never tire of this incredible Well of Wisdom. She was hurting. Devastated. Starving. She was one meal from death.

That is when a man of faith was sent into her life.

He did not criticize her, coddle her, or sympathize with her. *He knew how to get her out of trouble.*

She had to listen to him. She had to discern that he was a man of God. She had to be willing to follow his instructions, regardless of how ridiculous and illogical they appeared to her natural mind.

A man of God often holds the Golden Key to our financial deliverance. If you respect that anointing, the chains will fall off. Blindness will disappear. Your eyes will behold the golden path to blessing. If you become critical, resentful and rebellious, you will forfeit the most remarkable season of miracles God has ever scheduled into your life.

Nobody can discern a man of God for you. You must do it yourself.

Nobody can force you to obey a man of God. Your heart must be soft and broken enough before God enough to follow.

You may only receive one opportunity to obey the instruction that brings your deliverance. (Nabal only received one opportunity to feed and bless the army of David.)

You must recognize greatness when you are in the presence of it. It will not always demand attention. Jesus visited many places where He was undiscerned, undetected and unrecognized. His own family did not recognize His mantle, His Assignment, and that He was the Son of God. He did come into His own and His own received Him not.

You may have to find the man of God before he blesses you. You see, he is not needing you. You are needing him.

Read the incredible story of Saul and his servant, who had lost their donkeys. They were so disturbed until the servant remembered that a man of God lived in the area. He knew the power of an offering. They both made the decision to find the Prophet Samuel. The rest of the story is absolutely incredible. When they came into the presence of Samuel, the anointing from Samuel began to flow toward them (see 1 Sam. 9:3-10:10).

They had brought their Seed.

They brought an offering.

They believed he was a man of God.

That encounter with Samuel catapulted Saul into the kingship of Israel.

Somewhere, there is a man of God with the golden key to your house of treasure. Your responsibility is to discern it, find him and obey the instruction.

Several years ago, my Travel Assistant listened to me share the miracle of the "Covenant of Blessing," the sowing of the $58 Seed..."The Craziest Instruction God Ever Gave Me."

Now, my assistant was a fine young man who loved God. But, something happened as he listened to me tell the story. I instructed him and others in that service to give their Seed "an Assignment." "Write on the back where you want to experience the harvest in your own personal life," I instructed.

He wrote his $58 Seed, and then wrote on his check, "Better family relations." Here is what happened following that Seed:

1.   His mother came to Christ within 14 days.

2.   His two sisters came to Christ within 14 days.

3.   His daughter came to Christ within 14 days.

4.   He got to spend a week with two of his other daughters that he had not even seen in five years.

5.   He was able to have a meal and afternoon with his entire family—this had not happened in the previous 15 years.

6.   His 86 year old father came to Christ within 90 days.

7.   His oldest sister, who had run away from home 48 years prior, was located and came back home for a family reunion. (Nobody had seen or heard from her for 48 long years. She was considered dead.)

Every one of these miracles happened within 90 days of his sowing his Seed of $58.

Why? He followed the instruction of a man of God. Almost everywhere I go, I ask those who need miracles to plant a Seed. A specific Seed. Usually, I ask them to plant a Seed of $58. (Sometimes it is more, depending on the instructions of the Holy Spirit). The miracles are incredible. I get letters from everywhere relating the supernatural intervention of God following their acts of obedience.

A woman in Knoxville, Tennessee, approached me with a tall husband by her side. "Remember that $58 Seed?" she asked.

"Yes."

"This is him!" He was away from Christ and within a few days after her Seed, he came with her to church and gave his heart to God.

Those God sends may not be packaged like you anticipated. John the Baptist had an appearance many could not tolerate. But, God was with him. God's best gifts do not always arrive in silk. He often uses burlap bags to package his best prizes. Men do look on the outward appearance, while God looks on the heart.

Those God sends into your life may have harsh or uncomfortable personalities. If you could have heard Isaiah or Ezekiel, you might be shocked at some of the strong language that poured from their lips.

Those God sends with a special challenge to your faith may not appear socially fit. God often uses foolish things to confound the wise. You will not discern them through the hearing of the ear or the seeing of the eye.

You will discern them by the Spirit of God within you.

"Believe in the Lord your God, so shall ye be

established; believe His prophets, so shall ye prosper" (2 Chr. 20:20).

When you begin to acknowledge the Word of the Lord coming from proven and established servants of God, the flow of miracles will multiply and increase toward you.

You, too, may receive a "crazy instruction" from the Holy Spirit at some point in your life. Embrace it. Treasure it. It will become the Golden Key to the Harvest you have dreamed of for a lifetime.

The Proof Of Disorder
Is Pain.

-MIKE MURDOCK

∼ 12 ∼

Consider The Losses Your Rebellion May Create.

———————

God Will Not Force You To Follow His Crazy Instructions.

I remember hearing a minister preach in Honolulu that God will permit you to fail...to disobey Him. It seemed so strong to me at the time. As I thought on it, I had to admit that it was true.

God permits you to choose His way or your own way.

When you receive an instruction from God, it is wise to consider the losses your rebellion can set in motion in your life.

Rebellion is punished. Always. The law of consequence may not be apparent today. But, it is always inevitable.

Each Seed of disobedience is a magnet attracting a parade of tragedies into your home and life.

That's one of the dangers of mercy. Mercy is a very dangerous climate in your life. When God extends mercy, it can easily be misinterpreted and distorted in your mind and heart. Many think, it must not be that important. *I rebelled and nothing happened. No judgment. No losses. No consequences.*

Nothing could be further from the truth.

Delayed Consequences Reveal The Compassion Of God. "And the Lord passed by before him, and proclaimed, The Lord, The Lord God, merciful and gracious, longsuffering, and abundant in goodness and truth, Keeping mercy for thousands, forgiving iniquity and transgression and sin, and that will by no means clear the guilty; visiting the iniquity of the fathers upon the children, and upon the children's children, unto the third and to the fourth generation" (Ex. 34:6,7).

"Which sometime were disobedient, when once the longsuffering of God waited in the days of Noah, while the ark was a preparing, wherein few, that is, eight souls were saved by water" (1 Pet. 3:20).

"The Lord is not slack concerning His promise, as some men count slackness; but is longsuffering to us-ward, not willing that any should perish, but that all should come to repentance" (2 Pet. 3:9).

God Will Never Advance You Beyond Your Last Act Of Disobedience. The great leader had a tragic lesson in this at the battle of Ai. Achan, one of his sons in the Lord, attempted to cover up his own sin. God reacted. The Israelites lost the battle. Joshua cried out to God for an explanation of their great losses. God responded and told them to stop praying, to get up and to remove the sin that was in the camp. The stoning of Achan and his family is one of the most tragic scenarios in the Old Testament.

God is not stupid, not blind, not too busy to respond to rebellion. He sees. He knows. And sooner or later, He reacts to your rebellion. You cannot afford the losses a single Seed of rebellion can create. "Then shall they call upon Me, but I will not answer; they shall seek Me early, but they shall not find Me: For that they hated knowledge, and did not choose the fear of the Lord: They would none of My counsel: they despised all my reproof. Therefore shall they eat of the fruit of their own way, and be filled with their own devices" (Prov. 1:28-31).

Every tragedy can be traced to an ignored or unknown instruction. "There is a way which seemeth right unto a man, but the end thereof are the ways of death" (Prov. 14:12).

God promises gain to the obedient. He also guarantees loss to the disobedient. "If ye be willing and obedient, ye shall eat the good of the land: But if ye refuse and rebel, ye shall be devoured with the sword: for the mouth of the Lord hath spoken it" (Isa. 1:19,20).

Any Seed of Rebellion will produce disorder in your personal life. Order Is The Accurate Arrangement Of Things. Your car belongs in the garage. Your clothes hang orderly in your closet. Order is the obsession of God. Every instruction He gives you is intended to increase order in your life. His instructions are stepping stones to the greatest desires of your life and heart. So, when you ignore His instruction, you create disorder.

The Proof Of Disorder Is Pain.

Obedience increases order. Remember, order is the accurate arrangement of people and events in your life. *When you increase order, you increase your productivity, pleasure and profits.* "Let all things be done decently and in order" (1 Cor. 14:40).

Disobedience reveals disrespect of God and documents that you do not fear God. Fearing God means to honor Him and have a healthy respect for

His opinions, instructions and plans. God honors those who fear Him. He has promised incredible success to anyone who does fear Him. The fear of God is a catalyst for all Wisdom flowing from God. It is the trigger that releases the flood of blessing. "The fear of the Lord is the beginning of Wisdom:" (Ps. 111:10).

"Let us hear the conclusion of the whole matter: Fear God, and keep His commandments: for this is the whole duty of man. For God shall bring every work into judgment, with every secret thing, whether it be good, or whether it be evil" (Eccl. 12:13,14).

Whatever the price, obey God.

Obedience pays. That's the real secret to "The Craziest Instruction God Ever Gave Me!"

If you never do it again...sit down now...plant your Seed of $58 today. I strongly recommend that you plant an extra one for each member of your family. Focus your Seed toward the four Harvests of Isaiah 58: 1) Uncommon Health, 2) Uncommon Wisdom, 3) Uncommon Financial Favor, and 4) Uncommon Family Restoration.

Wrap your faith around the $58 Seed. Speak an Assignment for it. Do this only in total obedience to the Holy Spirit. Expect an Uncommon Harvest.

My prayer for you: "Holy Spirit, nobody can buy a miracle with money. But, everyone can sow a Seed of Faith in obedience to Your voice and expect an Uncommon Harvest from that Seed. I agree with my friend that this Seed of $58 will schedule the miracle Harvest needed most right now. Confirm this with signs and wonders according to the faith of the Reader today. It is done according to Your will. In Jesus' Name. Amen."

$58 SEED TESTIMONIES
It Can Happen To You!

Rent Paid For 6 Months

When I was at your meeting in Dallas, I planted a $58 Seed. In 58 days, I received a receipt stating that my rent was paid in full throughout the lease of six months. Looking forward to seeing you. Sandra - Tulsa, OK

10 Year Battle With IRS Ends!

We want to say that when I sowed the $58 Seed when you came to our church that week, a ten year battle with the IRS that had put us out of business came to an end as we suddenly won our medical hardship case with enough of a refund to even pay off our lawyer! Jerald and Roberta - Casey, IL

$58,000 Harvest!

You know, I completely forgot last year you had a dinner for partners at the airport. I sowed $58, it was November or October — can't remember — however, it was the first time my new company got a contract from a convenient store in December. That one store alone left us with $58,000 we sent you and many other ministries $58 and blessed my home assembly. Pastor Cheryl - Garland, TX

New Van!

In July, I responded to your $58 "Covenant of Blessings." I sowed the Seed on July 26th and the Lord blessed tremendously.

The Lord blessed my husband with a new van. We were able to visit my father together. Also, against company policy, I received full refund for airline tickets that I had purchased. We had decided to drive and not fly since we had a van. God also showed Himself strong with my husband. He took a test at work for another job — higher paying — and passed it with flying colors.

Loretta - Gary, IN

Childless Couple Receives Baby Boy As "The Harvest!"

In the Fall, we planted a $58 Seed-Assignment to have a child. We had been told by three specialists that I couldn't have children. Nine months later I had a 9 lb. 4 oz. bouncing boy.

Hallie - No City, State

$14,000 Miracle!

I had sent in a check for $58 on the 58 Covenant of Blessings. That day we received a check for $5,000 in the mail and a promise from my in-laws to pay off the rest of our land... mortgage at the bank for over $14,000. Praise the Lord!

Carol - LaPorte, IN

Income Increases 100 Times The Size Of $58!

Over the last two years, God led both of us out of our full-time jobs. We attended the Sunday, February 14, service in which Mike Murdock ministered. In response to his message about the 58 blessings and the offering which was taken, we dedicated our offerings for our family and for our own financial assistance. Mike Murdock said that we would see the answer within 58 days. Monday night, God's answer came "suddenly." We received a surprise telephone call that offered John full-time work for a project through the end of summer, the projected income is more than what John figured he would have to earn for us to be able to meet our needs for the entire year! By the end of the project, the income will be 100 times that of our offering. God is indeed good and really DOES multiply your Seed! Monday was Day 50 since Mike Murdock ministered and John starts work on Day 57!! Praise the Lord!

John and Christine - Plainfield, IL

Protection In Auto Accident!

I met you here in New York several months ago, and I planted a $58 Seed then and God has blessed me. On August 15th, I was in an automobile accident. The car flipped over twice, I think, but I am still alive and didn't suffer any injuries. Praise God.
Angela - Bronx, NY

New Car!

I attend church in Sarasota, Florida. You were here at the beginning of this year and asked for a $58 Seed.

I have been believing for a new car for some time now. I sowed a Seed and thirteen days later someone came to me completely unexpected and said they would buy me any car I wanted.

Our Youth Pastor was also blessed with a car and another single lady in the church had the same blessing (these are just the ones I know about.)

Thank you for being a part of the "new car" anointing here at Victory. God bless you and your loved ones.

Diane - Bradenton, FL

Given A Car!

We pledged $58 per month to a Christian television telethon and you were the guest speaker. This was a 12 month pledge — we believed God and He provided the money. "The pledge was paid off" about that time we were trying to sell our used car and purchase an $18,000 car. The owner said he would finance the deal himself. We were called to the owner's home to close the deal. Well! The owner and his wife told us the conditions for the deal had changed. They said God had impressed them to give us the $18,000 car and take the $3,000 down payment and put it in a savings account for our 6-year old son's education.

Larry - Broussard, LA

Changes In Alzheimer's Disease!

When you were at our church in Baltimore, in March of this year, I planted a $58 Seed for my mother's health and well-being. She will be 97 years old on May 27th and the doctor said Alzheimer's. We did not accept that diagnosis. About three weeks ago, we began to see and hear such a dramatic change in my mother that I know, and my family agrees, that God moved on her behalf. We expect her to have many more fruitful years.

Barbara - Baltimore, MD

Salvation Of Husband!

I sowed $5.80 three weeks ago, I received a $249 check, now I am sowing $58 x 2 ≈ $116 in my church, and I gave a command to my Seed for the 1,000 times more.

Today my husband received the Lord in my church in Vega Baja, this is one of the miracles I was looking for in 58 days.

Nelida - Puerto Rico

New Job After 3 Months Of Unemployment!

I sent $58 awhile back for my husband who had not worked in 3 months. He now has a good job!

Doris - College Station, TX

Marriage Healed!

My daughter and her husband were having severe marital problems and headed toward a divorce. The Lord had me plant the $58 Seed-faith for the restoration of lives to Jesus and to each other. My daughter took the children and went on vacation on Monday, the week after I was there for a week. She has returned and moved back in with her husband. I am most grateful and am believing for a whole lot more. Thank you for your Wisdom in the Word.   Arlene - Nashville, TN

From $50,000 A Year To $80,000!

My husband and I heard you speak about the $58 blessing on T.V.

The first month we named the Seed for our younger son. He went from $50,000 a year to $80,000 income change in one day basically. He took a random phone call at work from a headhunter and changed jobs. Anyone could have answered that phone!   Mary & Gary - Farmerville, TX

$10,500 Raise

Last year, I planted a $58 Seed after learning about the Covenant of 58 Blessings. I needed more income. In less than one month, I received a $10,500 raise. That was a 30% salary increase for me!   Rhonda - Arlington, TX

Income Increases 100 Times The Size Of $58!

The Holy Spirit moved me to sow two special $58 Seeds, and to believe God for 58 special blessings. I sowed a Seed for myself and wrote on the check, "Better Family and Life Relations." I sowed a Seed on behalf of my husband, and wrote on the check, "Better Family and Life Relations."

My husband found out that he had "unclaimed property" that had been turned into the State. The State of Texas sent him a check for over $1,100.

He got a tax refund check of over $8,000 delivered this week.

My dad, who had a stroke in December, has had his speech returned and he is up and can walk with a cane now. His mental facilities are intact and he is in good emotional condition.

My mother, who was in an auto accident, was told she needed surgery to correct the damage to her arm and shoulder joint. As of this week, the doctors are absolutely amazed at her progress. The woman is out using a chainsaw to cut down overgrown trees!   Jerry & Kim - Houston, TX

$10,000 Harvest!

I planted a $58 Seed and placed "Covenant of Blessings" on it. On January 14, my brother-in-law gave me a cashier's check for $10,000.   Rhonda - Houston, TX

Business Explodes!

My wife Carolyn and I recently had the pleasure of hearing you teach at our church. After the service, I purchased one of each of your tape ministries. Each of the tapes that I have listened to have been a blessing to me. At the service, we tithed $58 for every member of both mine and Carolyn's family. God's blessings continually flow out upon our family. Through your teaching of God's word, the Holy Spirit has revealed to me my Assignment in life. That is to support ministries in spreading the Gospel of Jesus Christ such as your own.

God had blessed Carolyn and I with a business that I started in 1987. In 1992 we almost lost everything we owned until we truly got ahold on the power of giving before you can receive your harvest. The company has now grown into the central warehouse for two major car manufacturers for the majority of the parts necessary to build these cars.

Thank you, and God bless you!

Bud - Springfield, MO

$700,000 In Real Estate!

You've done a great job. My life turned around 2 years ago after I saw you on T.V. talking about a $58 Seed-faith investment. I had $100 to my name, but I decided I'm poor anyway, so I sowed $58. I immediately saw increase and I now own over $700,000 in real estate and sow Seeds into 10 ministries. Thank you for showing me the way.

Rich - Melbourne, FL

Puerto Rico Miracle!

I'm writing you this letter to give you my testimony of the $58 Seed that I sowed when you visited our church in Puerto Rico. I lost my job on January 29, from this date to April 5, I was declaring the Word of God for a new job, but nothing happened. It was when I sowed the Seed when the miracles came true. On April 5, I started on a new job, better than the one I had! Lyzette - Rio Grande, PR

From Temporary To Permanent Employment

My letter is one more testimony about God's grace. About two months ago, Dr. Mike Murdock came to our church and asked the believers to offer a Seed of faith for $58. I was hesitant, because I did not have this money in my account, but in faith I seeded this Seed and I asked him to deposit it the day I was getting paid from my temporary assignment. After 58 days, I got a permanent job.

When my present boss interviewed me, this was going to be a temporary-to-permanent job, and when he offered me this job as his executive assistant, he gave me more money than I had asked. I was so afraid to ask for a higher amount of money, that I told him a lower amount. And he added, "I will hire you permanently, as it does not make any sense to pay additional moneys to the temporary employment agency. Also, I want you to enjoy the company's benefits." Lisa - Irvine, CA

New Job On 58th Day

I planted a $58 Seed for my husband to get a job...John started working — the 58th day! Glory to God!! Thank you for your teaching.   L. - Maywood, IL

Husband And Entire Family Born Again!

You asked for a $58 Seed offering, I felt moved to write a check, I couldn't explain why or my feelings, for I didn't know of planting Seeds or understand this "Seed Offering." At this time, I was Catholic and had been a Catholic for 49 years. My husband Cody freaked out, he called Pastor Young when we arrived home to let him know that he felt like he had been "conned." Well, needless to say, the Holy Spirit took over from this point, Cody, Samantha, Sebastian and myself became born again three weeks later. It was so very easy for the children and me, but for Cody, the Holy Spirit worked hard, satan did all he could to pull him away from God. But we serve a Big, Big God, it didn't take very long before Cody started making a 90 degree change, he now serves God with all his heart and soul. I am sure God sits on his throne laughing at my Cody in a sweet, delightful way for you see my Cody was one of the biggest Con Artists this area had the pleasure to see change and I thank God daily for these changes!   Barbara - Ladson, SC

Rent Miracle!

In October, I gave $58 for a financial miracle. I was two months behind on my rent, by the 60th day I received enough money to catch up on my rent and have a great Christmas. It really works! *Sheree - Long Beach, CA*

Free Car!

I had received your letter last Friday. I really felt impressed to sow a Seed. Your $58 Seed has really caused favor on my life. I'm a single man with two girls, now 13 and 9 years old. You came to our church last year...I sowed then in need of a job, car and home. You said sow the $58 Seed. I did out of my need — I needed a way home. My friend said she would take me home. To my surprise, at 10:00 p.m. at night, on Tuesday the end of May, I sat down in the car, my friend looked at me and said this is yours. I looked at her funny. She said it again. I thought she was joking. It was dark. He sat down in the backseat, I met him for the first time. I had been believing for a miracle. No one would finance me because I had no full-time job, just a temporary agency. Then I said ok. I was crying so hard. I thought finally they are going to do the financing. I became calm enough to say how much? She took my hand, laid the keys in my hand...it had a cross on the key ring and said "PAID IN FULL." *Kozette - Oakwood, GA*

$4,000 Debt Cancelled

We sowed four $58 Seeds...and God cancelled a $4,000 debt and paid off our truck. Thank you for showing me the blessing of sowing Seeds. Paul - Little Rock, AR

61 Year Old Husband's Salvation!

I sent you $58 —for my husband's salvation. He is 61 years old and has always been very grouchy and miserable all his life —sure enough! He's gotten saved and is now the softest, most gentle man. Shelby - Daytona Beach, FL

Meets Husband-To-Be

You spoke at a Singles Retreat in Tulsa. You taught on The Assignment and planting a $58 Seed. I had not understood the principle of Seed planting and was told it was a way of preachers and evangelists of getting into your pocket. But I was impressed to try God, if it didn't work I hadn't lost because I could still deduct it from my income tax. So I sowed $58 believing for a husband. I counted 58 days which was Aug. 11th. Two weeks later I met someone I hadn't seen in 10 years. (I moved to Tulsa from Iowa. This man taught at a Bible Study I attended IN IOWA 10 YEARS AGO.) We met for coffee/ice tea after church and also co-leaders of praise for a Bible Fellowship group. Well, the cafe saw us often and only for tea and our talks lasted a couple of hours. Needless to say, on the 52nd day we both knew the inevitable. We were married Thanksgiving Day. No one can tell me Seed planting doesn't work, and I have planted many more Seeds. Shirley - Tulsa, OK

Deliverance Of Smoking Habit

I sowed a $58 Seed several months ago for my husband, Richard, to quit smoking, he had tried everything for years. After sowing this Seed God has delivered him. Thank you for your obedience to God in sharing the Wisdom and Power in the $58 Seed.   Richard & Rosalyn - No City, State

A Widow With 8 Year Old Son Gets $$

I am a widow with an eight year old son. I have sowed a lot of Seeds with a lot of ministries, but your ministry (Glory be to my Father!!) changed my life. I sowed $58 for the 58 promises that God has for us. You told us to mark on our calendar 58 days. The first of my harvest was my 8 year old son telling me, "Momma, I know you are having it hard and I am going to stand with you, besides Momma, Christmas is Jesus' Birthday, that's the real reason." I said, "Lord 57 days ago I sowed a Seed and Mike Murdock told us to watch God move expecting." Before I could finish my prayer a co-worker walked over to my desk and gave me an envelope so packed with money I was too happy in the Lord to count it.

We love you and will always support your ministry.

Dec. 10 they gave me $300. And they told me they had more to come. I will write back and tell you the complete total, pressed down, shaken together, running over. I thank God for you, Mike Murdock.   Life - Winston-Salem, NC

A New House For $50,000

I must tell you this — a lady friend of mine gave you a $58 blessing covenant. And listen she got a new house for $50,000.00 at no cost to her not long after. Her name Is Reinelle. There's more to the story, yet she remembers that she planted a Seed at one of your meetings. *Regina - Kenova, WV*

A Couple Separated For 50 Years Remarried!

Praise the Lord, I'm shouting the Victory. I sent you a $58 check for a Covenant Blessing and, one week from the date I sent the check, I got a call from my first husband. I left my husband when my daughter was 3 months old. It has been fifty years since I saw him, and he called me and wanted to come and visit me. He came and we got things sorted out. He has gone back to Michigan to sell his home and come back. We are getting married again. *Fawn - Bismark, AR*

Christmas Bonus

I wrote out a check for $58 that night knowing I didn't have the money, but would be paid on the 27th and this check would exhaust my funds completely. Well, today is payday and not only did I receive my usual $219.33, but got a Christmas bonus check early for $423.66! Praise God! I just started crying!! *Jean - Streetman, TX*

Business "Takes Off"

Ever since I sent you a check for $58 my business has been taking off.   Joan - Des Moines, IA

Salvation Of Husband

The Holy Ghost truly took a great hold of me that day I was led to sow this $58 Seed for my husband's (Jimmy) salvation. I'm happy to say that as of March 2, he decided to accept Jesus as his personal Lord and Savior.

Yolanda - Orange City, FL

Child Support Jumps From $46 A Week To $600 A Month!

On Sunday, you asked the congregation to Seed a gift of $58, which I did, plus $40 extra. On the following Tuesday, we received a notice from our bank that our escrow account had been overpaid and they would be returning a check for $422.16. The following week my insurance company didn't charge me the usual $250 deductible for a painting accident that involved my neighbor's car. My son's child support payments will change from $46 a week to $600 a month. What a mighty God we serve!   Lolita - Lithonia, GA

$58,000 Miracle Harvest From A $58 Seed

Praise the Lord! We met in the Tampa airport in July. You were coming for a service and I had my picture taken with you and planted a $58 Seed. I have received $58,000 last month.   *Tommy - Tampa, FL*

Son And Grandson Re-United!

About a year ago...you spoke of the 58 blessings. I got excited about giving and convinced myself I could do it. I did send the $58 in several times. On one of the checks I put two of my sons' names. One of them was Dean. He was an alcoholic and my daughter was raising his son. Now, he and his eleven year old son, Eric, are back together. They live in Pontiac, Illinois. And, he has a job.   *Evelyn - Gary, IN*

Pregnancy Miracle!

The Lord spoke to me and told me to take one of my $58 per month Seeds...and sow it for her. Been praying three years for her to become pregnant. On 3/22 I sowed the Seed for her and told her to mark it as a memorial. On 5/28 she got her praise report, she is with child. Glory!!! Due date is 1/31.

Marcia - Deltona, FL

Free Building Given To Shelter The Homeless!

Two months after sowing $158 Seed, I was expecting for a miracle. One morning while in prayer, a man walked up to me and said I have a building for you. I have wanted a building for seven years and a place to sleep for men that have lost hope on life.

Thank God for encouraging me to sow the Seeds and God bless you.   Joe - No City, State

$14,754 Harvest!

We sent you a $58 Covenant check on March 15 for our finances. Clarence was disabled and had not worked for a little over two years and had been fighting for his benefits all this time.

We were so broke when we first heard your teaching that we made the decision to give the $58, but told the Lord we would have to have someone give it to us. This was a Friday night (March 14). On Saturday, someone did and we mailed it out on Saturday and counted off the 58 days on the calendar, which was May 12.

By May 9th, we received all his backpay benefits which totaled $14,754. Praise the Lord and thank you sincerely for your weekly teachings. God works! Plus our daughter and son-in-law got saved.

Just thought you might like to know.

Clarence - Salem, VA

Marriage Reconciled!

We sowed an uncommon Seed of $580 into your ministry and $1,000 into Pastor Cook's church. Praise God, my brother-in-law was saved after 20 years of prayer. My parents and my wife were reconciled after 23 years of my marriage.

Young & Judy - San Diego, CA

$91,110 Scholarship Is Harvest!

Praise God! I sowed a Seed of $58. My daughter was a senior in high school. But we were believing God concerning her college education. My income at that time was $201 a month. But praise God! Our Lord is a Supernatural Miracle Working God! My daughter received scholarships totaling $91,110. This is supernatural.   *Arnater - Chicago, IL*

New Floors & Carpet!

We had a water line burst in my house while we were gone. My whole downstairs was flooded. The outcome is that I have all new hardwood floors and my daughter, Shree', has new carpet. My whole downstairs is BRAND NEW! My insurance paid every dime of it. God is so good.

Joey sowed the $58 Covenant Seed and this was the outcome. Praise God.   *Penny - Mobile, AL*

Back Healed!

I planted a $58 Seed when you were in San Diego last month. You told us to write "uncommon favor" on the check. First, I received a healing in my back that same Sunday! Then, yesterday I got news that they are putting a traffic signal at a very dangerous intersection on the way to work. I have been praying for that for many years! Bodil - El Cajun, CA

$10,000 Miracle For Car!

I sowed a $58 Seed which was a sacrifice offering. I thought this will work. When you asked for $100 to be sowed, the sacrifice of faith came in! It would leave me with $7.34 in the checking account which is all I had. I did it. On the 44th day Provision on 5/11, I was blessed with 2 little kittens which doesn't sound important but it was to me and to God also. On 5/13 which was 46 Restoration, a man whom I did not know sowed a $9,000 Seed to get another car. He ended up sowing exactly $10,000. I now drive a 1993 Honda Accord LX (loaded) and he even gave me the color I liked. I have received uncommon blessings continually since then, airline tickets to see my grandbaby...extreme favor, Ezekiel 44:30.

I thank you for teaching me so much of the Wisdom that you have received, but this I will remember. "If What You Hold In Your Hand Is NOT Your Harvest, Then IT IS YOUR SEED." Pat - Sarasota, FL

Mortgage Harvest

You were on the telethon and told the story of the $58 Seed offering. I felt led to give. Well, Mike, in just 32 days I got my miracle. A man who owed me money on a mortgage for a house I had sold him, called to tell me he was going to pay it off. At this time he was almost 6 months behind. Even before this I received money that was owed to me from an investment that was made years ago. Sybil - Discovery Bay, CA

Marriage Miracle!

According to your advice, I planted a Seed of $58... believing something wonderful was going to happen for my daughter. I told her, "You are going to be the happiest person before the end of the year." I didn't know what it was going to be but BINGO just before Jan. 1 she met a wonderful man of God, fell in love and are now planning to get married soon.

Hirity - Plano, TX

A Parade Of Miracles!

I sowed a Seed of $58 for the 58 Covenant of Blessing. I have since been given a cute one bedroom trailer, a bed, a microwave oven, a student desk, a 19" color T.V., an air conditioner, and someone has offered to buy me a newer car in the next couple of months. Standing on His word brings tremendous results! Marsha - Baton Rouge, LA

Perfect Job 2 Weeks Later!

A while back I sowed $58 into your ministry and two weeks later I got the job I was hoping for.

Torre - Houston, TX

Leg Healed

The summer (June) I gave $58 love offering after reading "Covenant of 58 Blessings." I wrote in all four corners of my check what I needed from God. I had leg surgery in April, God saved my leg. Got 2 legs and 10 toes — all in good working condition.

My harvest so far:

My leg is healed — no more pain or swelling. Somebody sent me $300 in the mail. My wife got blessed with favor with her boss.

Jack - Donelson, TN

$924.65 Harvest!

On August 8, I planted a Seed for $58. After planting a Seed, I received a check in the mail for $924.65 from the insurance company. I called them asking what is it for. They told me they owed it, take it and spend it.

Mabel - Henryette, OK

Unexpected $2,250

I mailed in $58 in April and unexpectedly got $2,250 for our ministry.

Margaret - Big Rock, VA

In 58 Days - From $4.50 to $12.55 Per Hour!

I sowed $58 in April and counted 58 days... on the 21st day I was told that my job was sold. The good news is the company that bought it hired me and is now paying me three times as much. I went from $4.50 to $12.55 per hour! God bless.

Dyanne - Tulsa, OK

Relationship With Brother Is Restored!

I want to thank you for sharing with me "The Covenant of the 58 Blessings." So many blessings have been bestowed upon my life because I obeyed the Holy Spirit.

I planted a $58 Seed for my brother, my sister, and for a new home.

God has restored my relationship with my brother. Not only did God restore my relationship with my brother but, God blessed me with a new home 6 months after I planted the Seed. God also removed this boyfriend out of my sister's life. He was causing her a lot of financial problems and kept her from spending time with her children. Everything that I planted a Seed for God has blessed me with the answers to my prayers.

Cynthia - Clearwater, FL

Promotion On Job!

In December after giving the $58 covenant offering, my husband received a promotion on his job — in position and finance.   William and Cindy - Fairfield, CA

58% Salary Increase!

We planted a $58 Seed with a specific Assignment: that God would provide a new job.

My wife and I watered that Seed with prayers of thanksgiving and waited upon the Lord.

Twenty-three days into our Jubilee, I got a telephone call from the only company I sent out my resume to.

Forty-three days into my year of Jubilee, I was offered a position...of increase...of blessing.

Sixty days into my year of Jubilee I started that new job.

God's blessings: a 58 percent increase in salary, confirming God's involvement (remember the $58 Seed?). Stock options... less hours.   Neal - Bothell, WA

Daughters Receive Jobs!

Thank you and bless you for turning me on to the $58 blessing opportunity. God is so good! One month I wrote, "my daughter a job" on my check — both girls got jobs. How's that for a double blessing, not enough room for all my super blessings.
                    Marie - Weatherford, TX

10 Times Greater!

We sowed five $58 Seed gifts anonymously to a wonderful Christian man who happened to be in a severe state of depression. For a while we did not hear much about him, but God was at work to miraculously "heal" him, but found out he was back in Minnesota, getting married to a wonderful Christian woman. We were excited. But while God was doing this for him, He was busy selling a GRAIN BIN for us, that we thought could not be sold. It was sold and moved and my portion of the sale of the bin was over ten times greater than the Seed.   Wayne and Sheila - Minneapolis, MN

Son Delivered From Drugs And Depression!

I was impressed by the Lord to write a check out to you for $58.

Exactly thirteen days later my son, Kevin, who was bound by drugs, alcohol and suffering from depression over the loss of his sister, Sherri...was totally and completely delivered from it all instantly. Now he's on a spiritual high with God!

He said, "Mama, you've told me for eighteen years how good God really is, but I never really knew till now. Praise God," he said.   Ludez - Iva, SC

$4,600 Raise

I wanted to praise God for you and the revelation about the "Covenant of 58 Blessings" and the $58 Seed. I attended your Tampa conference in May. I planted a $58 Seed at that time and also stood for your prayer for those who did not have $1,000 to plant for the new Training Center, but who would give $1,000 if God provided it. I am praising the Lord because today I received the news from my boss that I am getting a promotion in conjunction with a $4,600 raise! July 17 would be 58 days, so the Harvest came in before the end of the 58 days! So I will be able to sow that $1,000 Seed for the Training Center. *Donna - Lakeland, FL*

Dad Gets New Job!

I sowed a $58 Seed of faith for my dad the evening you were at my church. My dad was out of work and he had a bad temper. Since I sowed the Seed, my dad has gotten a job and his temper has cooled down a lot. I thank the Lord! *Marlo - Anaheim, CA*

100-Fold Return!

I recently watched a replay of a telethon, you were talking of 58 blessings of God. The Holy Spirit moved on me to call. I had a stroke in April and was unable to use my left arm and had not worked since then. The next day, God sent a way to save my property. We also had a considerable amount of stock transferred to us; have started receiving Social Security for Disability after waiting 6 months. One blessing after another. The stock was exactly 100-fold! *T.E. - Winter Haven, FL*

6 Miracle Harvests!

I wrote one check for $58 — dedicated to "The Secret Place" as you suggested us to do.

I gave $58.58 in cash — dedicated to my daughter, who has had an incurable disease since the end of 1994 and is not living for the Lord.

The Lord multiplied $116.58 into at least $2,000.

My mother — who lives in Switzerland — sent me $150 for Easter.

Last Friday my 26-year-old daughter asked me to stop by. She gave me at least $350 worth of (expensive) clothes that were given to her she couldn't wear.

A lady gave me a beautiful bouquet of flowers for Easter at least $25-30 worth, because I allowed my 16-year-old daughter to help her out two weeks ago in an emergency situation.

The climax came last Friday afternoon when a company offered me a very special job with excellent pay. The Lord dropped the job "literally" into my lap. I didn't have to do anything — just show up.

Sunday I found out that I will get a refund check of over $1,500 from the IRS instead of owing them money — which was a total surprise to me. It appears to me that the Lord "opened up the windows of heaven!" Isn't that exciting!

Elisabeth - Dallas, TX

A Collection Of Incredible Harvests!

Seeded offering of $58. That same month, Jim went back to college to see if they would let him return to school. They advised him to change his major to Electronics and Computer Technology, then they would let him return. Also his grandfather paid all of his expenses.

The next month, he became engaged to the girl he met at college. Jim and Kim married, and both of them graduated from college on the same day. Today Jim is an engineer in Tulsa and works in a church, Kim playing the piano, Jim the organ and both teaching Sunday School classes.

Jeanene - No City, State

$20,000 Harvest

We heard you speak...sowed a Seed of $58. Within the next couple of months, we were given $1,000 from a few different people, a church and an anonymous giver. Praise God! I have made it through that most difficult time and my husband is now making about $20,000 and more in his business.

Janis - Elkhart, IN

Salary Is Doubled

Since I last sent your ministry $58 my life has been changed tremendously! My salary has doubled, instead of $1,200 bi-weekly, I am now earning $1,040 weekly!

Gloria - Charlottesville, VA

Children Are Testimonies To $58 Seed

So here is a little testimony to "the power of the $58." You spoke of the gift $58.

Our second oldest son did, in fact, graduate — in May and is now a youth pastor and coach at a Christian School. But while there, got on drugs and still lacks one semester for a degree in Pastoral Care. He called us last April for help. We brought him home and he was quickly delivered and is now here with us and preaching and ministering for God with a powerful anointing. Our fourth and last child is a ten-year-old son who is very strong for the Lord. So you see, Mike, God has done quite a few wonderful things since our Seed of $58.   Jerry - Pelzer, SC

Healing Is Harvest!

Last February, I was waiting for a miracle. I planted a Seed of $116 in your ministry.

I was put in the hospital. My doctor did a biopsy. It was cancer. I had thirty-six treatments plus two months of chemotherapy.

My doctor's report March 4, "JoAnn is without disease recurrence." Praise God.   JoAnn - Yountville, CA

Healing Of Chronic Depression!

My sister, Edna, was healed from chronic depression after Seeding $58 to you for her.   Gwen - Teaneck, NJ

Radical Changes From A Simple Instruction To Sow!

You talked about this revelation of the $58 Seed, it got me thinking, because I haven't tithed really good in church, but I always did give. Now, Mike, I live on welfare, my bills and rent come out to pretty close to what I get with just enough to usually get the boys something, plus I sponsor a child in Ecuador for $12 a month.

But here's what you told someone (me) that if we can't make ends meet now and then, that's the reason to give the Seed now. So, I thought, I don't need cable or long distance any more. That's Seed money.

Mike, I was saved before, but that day, the (Mark 1:8) Holy Spirit fell on me, and the Lord revealed to me what (Mark 4:21-23) I didn't really need in life.

Stamps are a lot cheaper. Mike, within 3 days of that Seed being sent, I got some furniture and things given to me which we desperately needed. Even a vacuum cleaner, which I was thinking two weeks before, going to buy used for $25. Then God personally delivered me to a Pentecostal church. I love this place.

I'm in school now for 20 hours a week. I'm going to Vo-Tech full-time starting in August for computer classes, all through Occupational Rehabilitation.

My 18-year-old son revealed to me, after putting his name on a money order, that he reads his Bible a lot at night.

Craig - Altoona, PA

96% Of Hospital Bills Paid Off!

I planted a $58 Seed.

Two weeks ago, God proved He was faithful. We had accumulated a little over $4,000 in bills at a local hospital. To make a long story short, I received a call two days later, telling me they had been able to write off 96% of our bill, which has left a balance of $163! *Deborah - Lima, OH*

Harvest Comes To Pastor Within One Hour

Wow! It has only been an hour or so since I dropped our first Seeds off at the post office. And within one hour we received $750 for the church. *Billy & Shanna - Jacksonville, FL*

1,000 Fold Return!

Thanks for the prayers. I sowed $1,000 into your ministry in Knoxville, TN. Also, I sowed a $58 Seed. Two weeks ago, negotiated a $58,000 cleaning contract. Let God be magnified. *David - Knoxville, TN*

Promotion With Double Pay!

Less than 58 days ago, I sowed a $58 Seed for finances. Always within 58 days God does something. Yesterday, I was offered a promotion at work which will double my weekly pay. This promotion is for sure "a desire of my heart."

Denise - Dallas, TX

Debt Cancelled After $58 Seed!

While you were with us...in Palm Springs, California, I sowed a Seed of $58 dollars to your ministry. One week later a debt that I owed of a thousand dollars was CANCELLED! My mother, who did not have $58 dollars at the time, gave $10. One week later she received a blessing of $5,100 and a nice increase in pay. I know that your ministry is true, and God has called you to be a Financial Deliverer for many, including me.

Joe - Palm Springs, CA

God Responds To 3 Seeds "Assigned" For Her 3 Children!

In March of this year, I planted a $58 Seed for each of my three children. Right away I could see a move of God's hand on their lives.

Now, my two teenagers are involved in youth for the first time, my oldest has been filled with the Holy Spirit and doesn't want to miss church anymore. All three are going to a Christian School and loving it. It had not been my plan, nor can I afford to send them, but I believe the desire and drive was sowed in us the day I sowed the $58 seeds for my children, to accomplish His will for their lives.

Cheri - Providence, KY

A Focused Seed For Daughter Unlocks Miracles!

As I was praying, He said, "turn the tape on." Just as I did, you were telling the story of "Melanie." And the exact words that I heard were, "plant a $58 Seed for Melanie." Melanie is the name of my daughter, who knew the Lord, but at the time was not walking with the Lord the way she should. Needless to say, I planted a $58 Seed! Gradually,… God turned her heart in a greater way toward Him. Thank you Jesus!

At the time I planted the Seed, Melanie was in serious spiritual and financial trouble. Several years before, she had been in a car accident and the case had dragged on all of these years. She had "no hope" of receiving any settlement from the accident. She won a court case concerning an injury in that car accident and was awarded a large amount of money!

Myrna - Phoenix, AR

3 Miracles Within 58 Days

Less than 58 days ago, I sowed a $58 Seed for financial increase, my own dwelling place and a car for my daughter. I am writing this letter from MY OWN APARTMENT, I received a dollar an hour raise on my job and someone at church gave my daughter a car! *Isabel - Denver, CO*

Raise Is 58%...From $58 Seed!!

This is my testimony of the $58 Seed: I had never grasped the concept of really wrapping my faith around my Seed before, so I had given significant offerings before, but I'd never had any significant return on them. You stressed the idea of believing that God would multiply my Seed if I would sow in good faith. And I believed. You said, "Count 58 days, and see if God won't give you significant blessings. Something will happen." And I waited.

<u>But I Believed That My True Father Would Do Something About It!</u>

On the 45th day my dad came home, so when he handed me my paycheck he said, "I really feel like we need to give you a raise." Praise God! But that's not the best part. I sowed a $58 Seed, not 25, not 50 — 58. Joe and I didn't figure this out for a couple of weeks after my raise. He got an idea —no doubt from the Holy Spirit! He said, "I wonder if your raise was 58%." He figured it up, and guess what?

My raise was 58%. I take home 57.59% MORE income now! God is so awesome! (I think He even set dad up for that one!)   Cindy - Barboursville, WV

JOIN THE
Wisdom Key 3000
TODAY!

Dear Partner,

God has connected us!

I have asked the Holy Spirit for 3000 Special Partners who will plant a monthly Seed of $58.00 to help me bring the gospel around the world. (58 represents 58 kinds of blessing in the Bible.)

Will you become my monthly Faith Partner in The Wisdom Key 3000? Your monthly Seed of $58.00 is so powerful in helping heal broken lives. When you sow into the work of God, 4 Miracle Harvests are guaranteed in Scripture:

► Uncommon Protection (Mal. 3:10,11)
► Uncommon Favor (Lk. 6:38)
► Uncommon Health (Isa. 58:8)
► Financial Ideas and Wisdom (Deut. 8:18)

Your Faith Partner,

Mike Murdock

□ **Yes Mike, I want to join The Wisdom Key 3000. Enclosed is my monthly Seed-Faith Promise of □ $58 □ Other $_____. Please rush The Wisdom Key Partnership Pak to me today!**

□CHECK   □MONEY ORDER   □AMEX   □DISCOVER   □MASTERCARD   □VISA

Credit Card # _____ Exp. ____/__

Signature _____

Name _____ Birth Date ___/___/__

Address _____

City _____ State _____ Zip _____

Phone _____ E-Mail _____

Your Seed-Faith offerings are used to support the Mike Murdock Evangelistic Association, The Wisdom Center and all its programs. The Ministry reserves the right to redirect funds as needed in order to carry out our charitable purpose.

Clip and mail completed form to:

THE WISDOM CENTER
P.O. Box 99, Denton, Texas 76202

1-888-WISDOM1
(1-888-947-3661)

Website:
WWW.THEWISDOMCENTER.

DECISION

Will You Accept Jesus As Your Personal Savior Today?

The Bible says, "That if thou shalt confess with thy mouth the Lord Jesus, and shalt believe in thine heart that God hath raised Him from the dead, thou shalt be saved" (Rom. 10:9).

Pray this prayer from your heart today!

"Dear Jesus, I believe that you died for me and rose again on the third day. I confess I am a sinner...I need Your love and forgiveness...Come into my heart. Forgive my sins. I receive Your eternal life. Confirm Your love by giving me peace, joy and supernatural love for others. Amen."

DR. MIKE MURDOCK

is in tremendous demand as one of the most dynamic speakers in America today.

More than 14,000 audiences in 38 countries have attended his Schools of Wisdom. Hundreds of invitations come to him from churches, colleges, and business corporations. He is a noted author of over 130 books, including the best sellers, *"The Leadership Secrets of Jesus"* and *"Secrets of the Richest Man Who Ever Lived."* Thousands view his weekly television program, *"Wisdom Keys with Mike Murdock."* Many attend his Saturday School of Wisdom Breakfasts that he hosts in major cities of America.

☐ Yes, Mike! I made a decision to accept Christ as my personal Savior today. Please send me my free gift of your book, *"31 Keys to a New Beginning"* to help me with my new life in Christ. *(B48)*

NAME   BIRTHDAY

ADDRESS

CITY   STATE   ZIP

PHONE   E-MAIL   B-151

Mail form to:

The Wisdom Center · P. O. Box 99 · Denton, TX 76202

1-888-WISDOM-1 (1-888-947-3661) · Website: www.thewisdomcenter.cc

DR. MIKE MURDOCK

1 Has embraced his Assignment to Pursue...Proclaim...and Publish the Wisdom of God to help people achieve their dreams and goals.

2 Began full-time evangelism at the age of 19, which has continued since 1966.

3 Has traveled and spoken to more than 14,000 audiences in 38 countries, including East and West Africa, the Orient and Europe. •

4 Noted author of 130 books, including best sellers, "Wisdom For Winning," "Dream Seeds" and "The Double Diamond Principle."

5 Created the popular "Topical Bible" series for Businessmen, Mothers, Fathers, Teenagers; "The One-Minute Pocket Bible" series, and "The Uncommon Life" series.

6 Has composed more than 5,700 songs such as "I Am Blessed," "You Can Make It," "God Rides On Wings Of Love" and "Jesus, Just The Mention Of Your Name," recorded by many gospel artists.

7 Is the Founder of The Wisdom Center, in Denton, Texas.

8 Has a weekly television program called "Wisdom Keys With Mike Murdock."

9 Has appeared often on TBN, CBN and other television network programs.

10 Is a Founding Trustee on the Board of International Charismatic Bible Ministries with Oral Roberts.

11 Has had more than 3,500 accept the call into full-time ministry under his ministry.

THE MINISTRY

1 **Wisdom Books & Literature** Over 130 best-selling Wisdom Book and 70 Teaching Tape Series.

2 **Church Crusades** - Multitudes ar ministered to in crusades an seminars throughout America i "The Uncommon Wisdo Conference." Known as a man wh loves pastors has focused on churc crusades for 36 years.

3 **Music Ministry** - Millions hav been blessed by the anointe songwriting and singing of Mik Murdock, who has made over 1 music albums and CDs available.

4 **Television** - *"Wisdom Keys Wit Mike Murdock,"* a nationally syndicated weekly televisio program features Mike Murdock teaching and music.

5 **The Wisdom Center** - The Ministr Offices where Dr. Murdock holds a annual School of Wisdom for thos desiring "The Uncommon Life."

6 **Schools of the Holy Spirit** - Mik Murdock hosts Schools of the Hol Spirit in many churches to ment believers on the Person an Companionship of the Holy Spirit.

7 **Schools of Wisdom** - In 24 maj cities Mike Murdock hosts Saturda Schools of Wisdom for those wh want personalized and advance training for achieving "Th Uncommon Life."

8 **Missionary Ministry** - Dr Mik Murdock's overseas outreaches to 3 countries have included crusades i East and West Africa, South Americ and Europe.